Born Again

Religious Exercise
or
Dynamic Experience?

Dr. Michael E. Dantley

Treasure House

An Imprint of
Destiny Image
P.O. Box 310
Shippensburg, PA 17257

"For where your treasure is
there will your heart be also." Matthew 6:21

ISBN 1-56043-808-8

For Worldwide Distribution
Printed in the U.S.A.

Inside the U.S., call toll free to order
1-800-722-6774

Contents

Treasure House books are available through these fine distributors outside the United States:

Christian Growth, Inc.
Jalan Kilang-Timor, Singapore 0315

Successful Christian Living
Capetown, Rep. of South Africa

Lifestream
Nottingham, England

Vision Resources
Ponsonby, Auckland, New Zealand

Rhema Ministries Trading
Randburg, South Africa

WA Buchanan Company
Geebung, Queensland, Australia

Salvation Book Centre
Petaling, Jaya, Malaysia

Word Alive
Niverville, Manitoba, Canada

Foreword

The literary work that you hold in your hand is not a sterile statement from a theological ivory tower, not the confining constructs of religious ritualism, but the burning flow of a heart after truth. Through this book, Pastor Michael Dantley takes us from the Nicodemian darkness of human endeavor into the glorious light of our second birth in Chirst. We rediscover the reality of our spiritual standing in observation of God's order as "He taketh away the first, that He may establish the second" (Heb. 10:9b). We are delivered from our depraved descension of the first Adam in our radical rebirth in the last Adam, Christ. Our greater inheritance is manifested in the transcendent transfer of the believer into the endless vistas of the Kingdom of God.

For too long the modern charismatics have sought depth in revelation through the shallow pools of their never-ending expression of "new things" (see Acts 17:21). Tragically, in our search for "the cutting edge," we have severed ourselves from "the simplicity that is in Christ" (2 Cor. 11:3). Many so-called "deep" Christians will dismiss a book written about the second birth as a field already picked clean by their active minds. Yet I believe this volume will yield tremendous treasures to those who truly hunger for spiritual reality.

Dr. Mark Hanby

Chapter 1

Introducing a Deeper Walk With God

Why is there such a variance between the principles of biblical faith and the way they are reflected through the life of the believer? Either the words of challenge, confrontation, and change that we find in the Scriptures are real possibilities for the believer, or they are the stuff of just another literary masterpiece.

The time has come for radical change in the life of the Church. The clichés, the traditional vocabulary, and the religiosity of the institutionalized culture that serve as the basis for religious activity and sustain foundational themes for believers, are destined for one of two fates. Either the folly they perpetuate will be exposed and they will be abandoned at the end of this era in Church history, or the substance of the true Christian walk will be seriously sought, revealed, and grasped.

Change is imminent because the Church is being forced to resolve the issue by answering the question, "Is the power of the Holy Spirit sufficient to produce a marked change in the life of the believer, or is the power of the Holy Spirit ineffectual?" If the answer is the latter, then the claims of the Church are fraudulent. Since I believe the power of the Holy Spirit is more than effectual, it is time for the Church to act to resolve this pressing dilemma.

The Church must abandon the fake and replace it with the genuine. It must stop presenting the defiled and offer that which is holy. Our spoken, as well as assumed, vision and mission must be carefully examined to determine if the Church is truly challenging its people to exemplify in their life styles the grave mandates of godliness as outlined in the Scriptures.

The seriousness of God and the winds of change are affecting the Church. The Church is being forced to carefully and critically consider the confessions and codes upon which its faith is built, maintained, and strengthened. The season has long passed when we blithely spewed forth biblical passages without also understanding their deeper meanings. The superficial and the mediocre are estranged from the seriously committed disciple of Jesus Christ. When we first entered the tabernacle, we found ourselves in the Outer Court. The Outer Court experiences produced limited knowledge that did not have the ability to sustain a relationship that calls each one of us into a deeper communion with the Lord. In the Outer Court we found the brazen laver, which was the place of ceremonial cleansing. It was through the water in this laver that we were cleansed of our carnality, a condition that was not permitted beyond this point. The Father would not accept offerings or sacrifices from priests with unclean hands.

The Father is longing for intimacy and serious fellowship with the people who belong to His priesthood, and this intimacy is found in the Most Holy Place. The unrighteousness, personal iniquity, and sin nature of the priest is disposed of in the Outer Court of the tabernacle. Then, and only then, is the priest prepared to move into the Most Holy Place.

In his book, *The House That God Built*, Dr. Mark Hanby writes that the laver was used for a very specific purpose. He outlines how the laver was positioned between the altar and the door of the Holy Place. This was indeed a strategic placement of the laver because, as Dr. Hanby writes:

...the laver represented priestly holiness and separation from the unclean, a cleansing of body as well as spirit.

Upon entering the priesthood, each priest washed "withal" at the laver; in other words, he washed all over. This certainly sounds like baptism, an act that follows the cleansing by blood. Once a priest had performed that first ceremony of cleansing and anointing for the whole body, the priest had only to wash his hands and feet when he entered the holy place of the tabernacle (the deeper things of God).[1]

---

1.   Dr. Mark Hanby, *The House That God Built*, (Shippensburg, Pennsylvania: Destiny Image Publishers, 1993), p.67.

Seldom do we hear of the prerequisites for an intimate relationship with God. If we glibly and carelessly prophesy, expound, and declare what the Lord is saying, our words will fail to propel men and women of God to enter a deeper communion with the Lord. Without the cleansing, the message lacks the power necessary to establish such a relationship.

Spiritual anointing, spiritual gifts, and divine commissions all originate in the Holy Place. It is essential for us to understand the bounty God has in store for us as we move into an ever deeper relationship with Him. But, if our understanding of the Word of God is retarded by arrogance, ignorance, flippant disregard, then even these sacred gifts cannot be maintained. In order for the Holy Spirit to teach us, we must divorce ourselves from the earthly nature that shrouds the concepts of traditional religion. We must permit the Holy Ghost to lead, guide, and teach our spirits. It is the Holy Ghost who discerns and reveals the path to the deeper walk.

The Holy Ghost will lead us beyond the false comfort of the rudimentary or elementary truths to which we have become accustomed. He will disrupt our cozy nest and plunge us into the depth of God's Word. The Spirit lights the way and helps us in our struggle with the revelatory truth of God's Word, which is so essential to a deeper, more serious walk with Him.

Those who desire the deeper walk will not be satisfied with, nor will they accept, the traditional walk. Driven by their desire for more, they will labor to follow the path of the Spirit and find rest only in the truth of the Word. No longer will they be pleased or satisfied with what has been established through tradition or human supposition. They are searching for the original interpretation and they will only be satisfied with an explanation of the Father's original intent, uncorrupted by religious institutions. They are not anarchists, but they are still revolutionary in their pursuit of God. The traditional interpretation of His Word is bitter in their mouths and cannot quiet the rumblings in their spirits. They seek the truth of God's presence for they want more of Him and less of what men and women have designed Him to be.

These people might be likened to the remnant the prophets mentioned. These people are so serious about their walk with God that they, like oil in water, separate from the rest in their pursuit for a deeper communion with the Father. They want more than a casual stroll. They want to *be* with Him. They long to repeat the communion Adam had with God before he sinned. If necessary, and if it be God's will, they will even settle for God's voice in their midst. They are aware of the shallowness of their fellowship with God and they know their current walk is missing the powerful presence of the Almighty. They have objectively assessed the areas of vanity and barrenness in their walk with the Lord and have correctly concluded that this type of communion, is at best, superficial. For those who would enter the deeper life, into His presence, He has established specific requirements and they realize they have not submitted to the requirements. In essence, they are not in agreement with God.

We must understand that, despite all of the grand theological treatises and all the worldly philosophies designed to reveal our purpose for living, our fundamental purpose is to walk in agreement with the Lord. The prophet says, "Can two walk together, except they be agreed?" (Amos 3:3) The New American Standard Bible translates this verse in this way: "Do two men walk together unless they have made an appointment?" The phrase "to make an appointment" comes from the Hebrew word *ya-ad*, which has multiple meanings. It means to be destined, set apart, meet, or come together. It may also mean purpose, mission, aim, or goal. When we apply all of these variant meanings to this verse, we gain a deeper insight into what it means to walk together in agreement with God. The Hebrew implies that those who accompany one another, walk together, and share their lives, are destined to do so if they are in agreement. This rendering of the verse provides us with deeper insight into what it means to walk in agreement with God. Implicit in our response to God's plan is a conscientious, deliberate decision to walk in intimacy with one another. In the end it is a mutual endeavor and each individual has carefully considered the options before starting down the path.

When we decide to accompany God, we must place demands on the flesh. We must resolve, after serious deliberation, to walk in agreement with the mind and heart of God. Please know that our agreement with God depends upon mutual understanding, a commonality of vocabulary, and a submission to God's intentions and purposes for our lives.

In order for us to walk in agreement with the Lord, we must submit ourselves to a process. Part of the process that leads to walking in agreement with God is called *confession.* Through the process of confession we rid ourselves of unwanted baggage and align ourselves with the thoughts and intentions of the Lord. In order for that to happen, we must come to know Him and His ways. As we learn more of Him and His ways, we will grow in confidence and our ability to hear and distinguish the voice of the Shepherd will increase. It is essential that we hear and understand what the Lord is saying if we are to be consistent in our communion with Him.

We must speak the same language as the Lord. We must define life as He defines it. Our concepts must be grounded in His revelation. If we are to move in the flow that He has initiated, we must be suspicious of those who would offer a way of thinking or a perspective that lacks the essence of the divine. We must seek His wisdom to provide our definitions. We must look to Him for the meanings of His words, for the concepts He wants us to embrace, and for the perspectives He wills for us to possess. Confession simply means that we willingly align ourselves with the passions of God so our vision is defined by what He sees.

We should mimic the behavior of the prophet Habakkuk and eagerly turn to see what the Lord will say. Our friendship with the Father begins as we progressively decrease and, through our decreasing, He begins to increase in us. Our confession says that we consent to the desires of God in every aspect of our lives. We gratefully relinquish the control of our lives and confidently transfer all authority to the Lord. We are confident that His original intentions for our lives will be accomplished with greater ease if we release ourselves into His awesome hands. Suddenly, we are aware that the eternal promises of God, once bound in a future time, are, potentially, a present reality. We discover that with Him there is no time, no past, and no future. God abides perpetually in the present and His original intention was for us to abide in His presence eternally.

For the time being, we must continue toward the future since we, though spiritual, are bound by the sands of time. Although we don't fully comprehend all that lies ahead and all through which we must pass, we know the journey will culminate in the demonstration of God's purpose or will for our lives. So we submit with assurance and confidence that Philippians 1:6 is true:

...He Who began a good work in you will continue until the day of Jesus Christ—right up to the time of His return—developing [that good work] and perfecting and bringing it to full completion in you (Philippians 1:6 AMP).

Don't confuse godly confession with fatalism. Walking in agreement with our Creator, who had a plan for our lives before we were conceived in the womb, means we know He is more than able to fulfill His promises and complete the process. The catechism of religious doctrine is no longer a sufficient foundation for our walk with the Lord. Those ideas are often void of truth and lack biblical authority. They are held together by human intervention and have not plumbed the depths of the revelation of God. They have no basis for the deeper, more significant spiritual walk the Lord intends for His people today. Those who are serious about their pursuit of God must be able to identify partial truths and misinterpretations that are offered for the message God wants to impart to His people. Those who refuse to settle for the domain of the religious must also refuse to walk in anything less than the present, progressive revelation of the whole truth.

Jesus said, "And ye shall know the truth, and the truth shall make you free" (Jn. 8:32). We cannot begin to live in the liberty God intends for His people until we come face to face with the truth—not denominational doctrinal statements, not sectarian creeds, not ecclesiastical treatises, but the *truth*. Understand, it is the truth and not the knowledge of the truth that liberates us. The truth releases us from the bondage that has enslaved our minds and hearts, our bodies and our spirits. Having only knowledge of the truth is nothing more than mental assent to the merits of veracity. That is merely an intellectual exercise, a form of mental gymnastics. Knowing the truth and walking in that truth, however, removes us from passive knowledge to active participation. This is the highest manifestation of truth.

A lie is not the only thing that enslaves or ensnares us. Perfunctory, superficial knowledge of the truth is also oppressive. When we possess only the aroma and not the substance of the truth, we lack power and purpose. We miss out on its efficacy and we are bereft of its virtue. We fail to enjoy the benefits the knowledge of that truth offers to those who would make the decision to live in it.

Historically, the Church has settled for a residue of truth; we have been satisfied with disjointed fragments or substitutes for truth. Because mankind has settled for less, we have forfeited our spiritual inheritance as well and allowed the Church to reign without power and authority. It even reigns under the guise that it is the true interpreter of God's will and intentions. The truth has been replaced with a lie, or at least, it has been reduced to partial truth.

The tenets of the world system are given free course in the Church because we have abandoned the foundational truths. We have incorporated the ways of the world into our walk with Jesus Christ and we have sampled the fruit of worldly philosophy and decided a subscription to those concepts makes more sense. We have deluded ourselves into believing the world's system is more rational than God's system for the Body of Christ. For the sake of convenience, we have replaced the true model with a shabby substitute. A mind that should be sound and focused on God's truths, is now filled with confusion. What it can't explain automatically becomes anathema to the Christian and the world system agrees with his assessment. By taking the road of least resistance, we leave the foundational truths of the Church bereft of credence, subjugating them to the realm of psycho-ethereal, impractical fantasies.

If the Church would dare to risk a search for the bedrock of truth, however, such an expedition would lead to the very throne room of God. Here it would find the awesome presence of God and, ultimately, be consumed by the fire of fellowship and communion with God.

It is no wonder that volumes are now being written to encourage believers to journey into the Most Holy Place. These books reveal a life style engaged in the authentic presence of Almighty God. Prophetic declarations are calling the people of God from mundane, mediocre religious experiences to take a seat with Jesus Christ in heavenly places. The traditional paradigm, which requires physical death before taking a seat next to Jesus, is no longer seen as valid. From this perspective the following discourse between Jesus and His disciples takes on new meaning:

> *Let not your heart be troubled: ye believe in God, believe also in Me. In My Father's house are many mansions: if it were not so, I would have told you. I go to prepare a place for you. And if I go and prepare a place for you, I will come again, and receive you unto Myself; that where I am, there ye may be also* (John 14:1-3).

Unlike the traditional interpretation of this text, which is generally filled with the notions of physical death followed by a future life in the presence of the

Lord, a radical approach to understanding this passage is to assume that Jesus is giving the disciples access to heavenly places during their earthly existence. Chapters one and three of Paul's letter to the church at Ephesus reinforce this interpretation. As disciples of Jesus Christ, we have permission and authority to sit with Christ in heavenly places. The way to do this is through the flesh of Jesus Christ. He is the way, or the instrument, or the key that unlocks the door and ushers us into heavenly places. He is the way, or the means, by which we access the warehouse of spiritual gifts in the heavenlies, gifts that have been prepared for our use.

This different interpretation or fresh revelation of the familiar text from John 14 comes out of a close communion with the Father. What happened is the Spirit of truth, of whom Jesus speaks, is moving in His office to guide the people of God into the whole truth. The traditional design will not suffice for those who are remnant believers. Half-truths and partial concepts will no longer satisfy the thirsty spirits of men and women who recognize the difference between the vanity of religion and the abundance of God. Bible verses, lifted out of context to offer false hope, cannot satiate the longing for God that pounds in their hearts. So the truth, free of worldly additions, must be proclaimed for men and women, the remnant people of God, to be set free to walk in His presence.

One aspect of God's truth that has been shrouded in mystery needs to be made clear to all: the doctrine of the second birth. By whitewashing the truth, we have hidden the substance of life with God and denied access to those who desire a richer, deeper communion with Him. We have relegated the second birth to a position of religious legalism rather than releasing the truth of the doctrine and thereby liberating those who are genuinely born again. It is the truth of the second birth that will set us free as we explore its depths and abandon the traditional trappings surrounding it. The purpose of this book is to uncover the truth regarding the second birth. As the truth is revealed and embraced, born-again believers everywhere will take their place under the authority that was established for them before the foundation of the world.

It is my prayer that, as you read these words, layers of hurt, pain, and disappointment will fall from your heart. As the burden is lifted your spirit will be free to dwell where it belongs. As you understand the second birth, the issues of your first birth will become clearer. Please read this book anticipating, at the end, that you will walk freely as the new creation your Father intended you to be, and enjoy the kingdom He prepared for you.

Chapter 2

Adjusting the Means to Reach the End

Essential to understanding the power of the second birth is struggling with what I call a *paradigm shift*. A paradigm is a model, mold or pattern. The paradigm establishes the parameters from which behavior is developed. It sets the norms or standards for thinking, believing, or perceiving. From the elements of the paradigm we can identify what is right and wrong, and what is to be the standard of thinking, conventional behavior, and the prevailing attitudes. As more and more people subscribe to the propositions of any particular paradigm, the boundaries of thinking, behavior, and attitude become more rigid. The paradigm grows from a set of guiding principles into established traditions through which the behavior of the culture is sifted and appraised. Ultimately, it stands as the measuring rod of the acceptable and sets the limits for determining the realm of the unacceptable. All that falls outside the paradigm is judged as heresy, anarchy, and rebellion.

Paradigms remain steady because systems of maintenance and reproduction are built within them. When a paradigm is first established, specific processes secure and guard its content. Like sentinels they engage all opposing thought patterns and ward off all attempts to tamper with or change the content of its foundational beliefs. A paradigm is not easily shifted and it is seldom discarded and replaced. But through intense struggle, often accompanied by mental, emotional, and physical violence, paradigms are changed or shifted.

The Church has accepted a paradigm of the second birth that strangles all of the life and vibrancy out of this Kingdom principle. We have bought into a narrow notion of being born again, placed it in the hands of religious fanatics and crazed fundamentalists, and through such subjugation, have reduced the power and weakened the life-changing substance of the second birth. The prevailing paradigm leaves people to struggle with areas of their lives that should have been resolved in the process of atonement. It causes Christians to wonder if the second birth is real or simply a cliché that is proclaimed to gain entrance into the religious system of the local church.

The traditional paradigm of the second birth, the one prevalent today, is so handicapping that it acts like a cataract on the spiritual eyes of the believer. Although the Church has accepted and promoted this traditional view of the second birth, there is another voice we need to hear. The Holy Scriptures challenge us to refuse to establish a permanent habitation in the status quo. By agreeing with such a system, we may well be forsaking the better plan the Lord has designed for our lives. Hebrews 10:9 in the Amplified Bible says this:

...Thus, He does away with and annuls the first (former) order [as a means of expiating sin] so He might inaugurate and establish the second (latter) order (Hebrews 10:9 AMP).

Throughout the Scriptures the Lord extinguishes or invalidates the status quo. He changes or modifies the prevailing paradigm to institute His will. Chapters 6 through 10 in Hebrews are filled with examples where the Father abandoned the first order to establish the second. In these chapters the writer explains that the Aaronic system for atonement and remission of sin was ineffective. The priests, using this system, failed to satisfy the righteous requirements of the Father. Still, the first priestly order had been established and ordained by the Lord. Exodus 28:1-3 in the Amplified Bible says this:

From among the Israelites take your brother Aaron and his sons with him, that he may minister to Me in the priest's office, even Aaron, Nadab and Abihu, Eleazar and Ithamar, Aaron's sons. And you shall make for Aaron your brother sacred garments [appointed official dress set apart for special holy services] for honor and for beauty. Tell all who are expert, whom I have endowed with skill and good judgment, that they shall make Aaron's garments to sanctify him for My priesthood (Exodus 28:1-3 AMP).

It is clear that the paradigm of the priesthood was established by God. It includes the following:

—specifications as to the persons to function in the priestly office,

—the purpose for the priestly office,

—the appointed dress while functioning in the office,

—the divinely established familial line upon which the priestly mantle was to remain, and

—the one to whom the priestly office belonged.

This paradigm operated with the authority of God. It received its life from none other than the I Am. God instituted the priestly office and He gave it purpose. He established the boundaries of the paradigm in such a way that there would be no question of responsibility and function for those who held the office. There should be no question that God clearly intended the elements just enumerated to be a part of the paradigm of the priestly office. The purpose of the Aaronic priesthood was to satisfy the righteous nature of God by offering appropriate sacrifices.

But the writer of Hebrews tells us that the paradigm shifted. Hebrews 7:11-16 in the Amplified Bible says this:

Now if perfection [that is, a perfect fellowship between God and the worshipper,] had been attainable by the Levitical priesthood, for under it the people were given the Law, why was it further necessary that there should

arise another and different kind of Priest, one after the order of Melchizedek, rather than one appointed after the order and rank of Aaron? For when there is a change in the priesthood, there is of necessity an alteration of the law [concerning the priesthood] as well. For the One of Whom these things are said belonged [not to the priestly line but] to another tribe, no member of which has officiated at the altar. For it is obvious that our Lord sprang from the tribe of Judah, and Moses mentioned nothing about priests in connection with that tribe. And this becomes more plainly evident when another Priest arises Who bears the likeness of Melchizedek, Who has been constituted a Priest, not on the basis of a bodily legal requirement—an externally imposed command concerning the physical ancestry—but on the basis of the power of an endless and indestructible Life (Hebrews 7:11-16 AMP).

The shift in the paradigm, as outlined in these verses, is as follows:

—the traditional priesthood that had been established by God was ineffectual in satisfying the Father's definition of righteousness;

—the customary method or process of fulfilling the priestly office only placed more ineffective men into an ineffective office;

—a paradigm shift was necessary to ensure that the Father's definition of righteousness and holiness could be achieved; and

—any trappings of the traditional priesthood's paradigm had to be obliterated so God's ultimate purpose could be achieved. The Aaronic priesthood continued to follow the instructions and the divinely instituted regulations, but there was no lasting effect.

Clearly, the paradigm of the priesthood changed. But just as clear is that, while God ordained and established the shift, He remained immutable. What is revealed in these verses is a God who is absolutely sovereign and who, motivated by the everlasting covenant He established with man, has sworn to maintain it. By shifting the paradigm, the Father took the revelation of His purpose, which is the manifestation of His will, and ensured its continued implementation.

Surely our Father did not change His mind, even though, as sovereign Lord, He could. No, instead the Lord assessed that extent to which His sworn covenant with man could be implemented through the existing structures and systems He had established. Through His analysis, He realized the earthly priesthood was ineffective. So, He replaced the original religious system with a better one and established a priesthood that was free from human intervention. This better priesthood lacked any ties to the traditional Aaronic line. There was no way to trace its origin through human genealogies and there was no evidence of its departure from the earthly realm. Through the resulting paradigm shift, the Lord established the priesthood on the order of Melchizedek and thereby brought to fruition His sworn covenant with man.

Oh, that we could understand the purpose and methods of God in bringing His purpose to pass.

The Lord of hosts hath sworn, saying, Surely as I have thought, so shall it come to pass; and as I have purposed, so shall it stand (Isaiah 14:24).

It is essential for us to know that because of the sovereignty of God, He is free to arrange and rearrange any one or all of the systems He has established. It is because of His great mercy, the Book of Lamentations proclaims, that we are not consumed. We must come to the realization that often the shifting paradigm provides us with the manifest mercy of God applied especially at our time of need.

The idea of the Lord annulling the first to establish the second is exceptionally compelling. The Lord allows, and even participates in, the process of establishing the first order. But, even though the first order had purpose, it is not the ultimate resolution. The Aaronic line and the first order of the priesthood served its purpose. It was the vehicle that affected the release of God's mercy toward mankind and manifested His mercy in the sacrificial death of Jesus Christ.

We must never look with disdain upon the first order. It had to be established. It propelled the birth of the second order and, in comparison, provides us with a way to understand the need for the second order. Out of the shortcomings of the old we see the marvelous fullness of the new. The first was replete with dysfunction and flaw. The second, however, is the completion of the original intent of the Father. Filled with His mercy and grace, it gives those who choose to accept the terms of His covenant the opportunity to live in the place He had prepared for them.

As the recipients of the Father's blessing through the paradigm shift, our position in His Kingdom is evidence of the truth of His purpose. To move from the old paradigm to the new paradigm can be compared to the Christian who progresses from glory to glory. In order for this glorious progression to occur, we must adopt a new way of thinking, perceiving, and behaving. To progress from glory to glory means to recognize and understand those experiences from which the initial glory flowed. It also demands that we release those experiences and avoid the tendency to establish them as spiritual tradition. If we are free to accept the shift, we open ourselves to flow in a new direction or to encounter a new set of experiences, as the Lord shows us the way into the next aspect of glory. Isaiah 54:2-3 reads thus in the New King James Bible:

> *Enlarge the place of your tent, and let them stretch out the curtains of your dwellings; do not spare, lengthen your cords, and strengthen your stakes. For you shall expand to the right and to the left, and your descendants will inherit the nations, and make the desolate cities inhabited* (Isaiah 54:2-3 NKJ).

These verses speak of a shift in the prevailing paradigm. They speak of enlarging, stretching, and expanding. By the mere definition of these three terms, the original status or the first condition must be annulled so the second, which often is God's original intention, may be realized. It was always God's plan for Israel and His people to reign.

The pollution of the flesh, carnality, and blatant disobedience delayed God's original design for His people. This, in turn, delayed them from walking in His perfect will. Because He was not pleased with the progress of their walk and their status in His plan, the paradigm shifted. As His original intent was reestablished with a shower of mercy, they found themselves walking in obedience. To enlarge, stretch, or expand one's borders demands that the status quo be jolted. The traditional must be disengaged and the mind-set of those who have been called to enlarge, stretch, and expand must be one of leaving and cleaving—leaving the old paradigm and cleaving to the better one.

Therefore, the Church must leave the realm of the comfortable, especially where the interpretation of the second birth is concerned. It must venture into the progressive revelation the Lord would have us embrace and understand concerning the second birth experience. It is my firm belief that, if we fully understand the whole notion of the second birth of John 3, those formidable, insurmountable issues that often seem to hinder us would have little or no influence on our lives.

Without a clearer understanding of this doctrine, Christians are doomed to lives of perpetual defeat and repeated calls for repentance for the same issues. Essentially, we are held hostage to the sin nature of our past rather than walking freely in the life of liberty and abundance the Lord has established for us. We will find the same sinful behavior rearing its head in our lives time and time again, causing us to question if we were ever redeemed.

Whether we want to admit it or not, this is a fundamental problem with many who have been saved through the precious blood of Jesus Christ. It is not that we are pretending to walk with the Lord. We simply have not been successful in throwing off the weights and the sin that so easily beset us. We are failing in this area of our walk because we have never really understood what it means to be born again. We have some knowledge of church membership and the process of salvation, but we do not really understand the power and the magnitude of our spiritual birth. Until we get to the place where we understand the significance of our spiritual birth; until the reality of the spiritual birth dictates the parameters of our behavior and thought patterns; until we allow the blessings that accompany the spiritual birth to consume us; we will forever live far beneath the original intent of the Father.

An intellectual understanding and acceptance of this concept cheapens the effectiveness of the spiritual birth. It minimizes and weakens the life-changing nature and purpose that the spiritual birth offers. Perhaps intellectual agreement with the doctrine of the second birth starts a walk with the Lord that whets the individual's appetite for intimacy. But it falls short in fully developing and releasing men and women to walk so they are conscious of the presence of the Lord. Only when one is conscious of God's presence do the barriers of theological jargon and religiosity that typify the mundane walk with Him fall away. For those who fail to experience a true, Spirit-filled acceptance of the rebirth, refreshment and restoration never come.

The Christian who walks with the spiritual witness of the second birth has renounced the empty customs and traditions of religious institutions and has an overwhelming desire to uncover the divine truth of the purpose, intention, and design of the Father. A walk that includes such commitment automatically shifts from the cavalier to the serious. It is recognized by an intensity that lacks superficial rituals, and instead plunges into the depths of the covenant relationship.

This is the essence of the paradigm shift. Only the remnant people—those who have sold out to the Lord, those who are serious about this walk, those who are the called-out ones—will dare to embark on the excursion into the depths of the second birth. The journey demands the sacrifice of traditional thinking, the release of a mind-set that perpetuates one's status as a prisoner to the religious traditions, and the release of a culture that swears the journey is ludicrous and worthless at best.

This paradigm shifting, where the second birth is concerned, is a serious undertaking. Nevertheless, it must take place before one is free to truly walk in the design and the purposes of God.

Chapter 3

Moving Beyond
the Natural

As we begin to consider the concept of being born again, the foundational Scripture for our study will be chapter 3 of the Gospel of John. Here we find the dialogue between Jesus and Nicodemus, which deals with this whole issue. A quick reading of this text often causes one to miss the importance of the meaning behind the words of Jesus. This was an intimate time of tremendous discovery between these two men. But first, consider the man Nicodemus.

The first verse gives some interesting information about this man's life. He was a Pharisee and a member of the ruling body. The Pharisees were a recognized sect of the Jews who were meticulous in their efforts to obey the laws of Judaism. The Pharisees stressed the need for all Jews to obey the smallest part of the law and all of its principles as recorded in the Old Testament. When the Jews were led off to a life in captivity in Babylon, the

Pharisees saw it as a direct result of the people's disobedience to the law of God.

They also established a formal system for teaching and studying of the Torah. In the course of their study, they added interpretations, which became supplements to the law. These supplements usually defined the law more strictly. That way there would be no possibility of misunderstanding its requirements, and thus breaking it by accident or ignorance.

As a ruler of the Jews, Nicodemus was a man of position, status, and authority. Perhaps it was because of his prominence that we find Nicodemus coming "at night" to talk with Jesus. Isn't it ironic that a man of such tremendous authority, power, and knowledge of the law would find it advantageous to come to this particular Rabbi? I think it is significant that Nicodemus chose to confer with Jesus while hidden by the cloak of darkness, when it would be difficult, if not impossible, for anyone to really know that he had an audience with Him. Scholars have suggested that Nicodemus came to Jesus at this time because in the daytime such an action would have been grounds for stripping him of his position, status, and authority. This simple act of seeking counsel with the Lord could have resulted in his dismissal from his position in the Jewish hierarchy.

There are several other interesting dynamics surrounding his visit. When Nicodemus speaks with Jesus, he uses the plural "we know." This may be an indication that others were with him—perhaps his entire family. With his background and cultural baggage, it must have been difficult for him to make the decision to approach the Lord. He surely had a comfortable life. However, he may not have been happy preserving the status quo. He undoubtedly had heard of the miraculous power of Jesus Christ and these miracles may have stirred him to find out more.

> ... *"Rabbi, we know that You are a teacher who has come from God. For no one could perform the miraculous signs You are doing if God were not with him"* (John 3:2 NIV).

Clearly, Nicodemus had been observing Jesus, for Nicodemus admitted that he was aware of the signs and wonders Christ had performed. He also admitted that no one could do such wonders without the presence of God in his life. Referring again to the use of the plural "we," it is obvious that he spoke for himself as well as for others. He declared that others, besides himself, knew that Jesus was a teacher come from God. They also understood that, in order for Jesus to have performed such miracles and signs, He had to have been directed by or intimate with God. With this acknowledgment, Nicodemus recognized and gave homage to the anointing of Jesus Christ.

To acknowledge the close relationship and communion between Jesus and the Father was an extremely deep declaration for Nicodemus to make. This man knew the law and was well acquainted with the Scriptures. He fully understood that Jesus had to have been closely aligned with the Father in order for Him to have accomplished what He had. So, fortified with his knowledge of Scripture and driven by a personal knowledge of the power of the Father, Nicodemus knew that Jesus was not the average Jew. He saw that Jesus was not a "run of the mill" rabbi. There was something special about Jesus—so special that Nicodemus had to come to Him to find out more about Him. Although Nicodemus came to Jesus seeking only information, he found himself facing a life-changing experience as he listened to the words of Christ.

"Life-changing" is an appropriate phrase to describe the encounter Nicodemus had with Jesus. Nicodemus had grown up in a strong traditional religious environment. In fact, where the Lord and the law are concerned, and because of his religious ideology, Nicodemus was a black-and-white, linear thinker who left no room for grace, ambiguity, or "self-interpretation." He was a man motivated by status and authority and yet, as these verses indicate, Nicodemus desired more.

So many of us can relate to this situation. We have discovered that a religious environment simply does not satisfy. Knowledge of the Father based on information and intellect leaves us wanting. It would seem that the more one learns about the Father through scholarly pursuit, the more one is caused to exchange intellectual reward for the passion of an intimate communion with the Lord. There comes a point where we yearn and hunger for more than an empirical examination of the Scriptures and a purely theological approach to the Lord. We desire to know Him!

Given the disclosure Nicodemus made regarding Jesus Christ, the Lord's response may seem somewhat puzzling. Jesus tells Nicodemus this in John 3:3:

...Verily, verily, I say unto thee, Except a man be born again, he cannot see the kingdom of God (John 3:3).

After further thought, Jesus' response really is appropriate when one considers the mind-set that drove Nicodemus to make his initial statement. He was saying that Jesus had to have come from God because of the signs and wonders He had performed. He is affirming that the Father must be with Him, otherwise such miracles would be impossible. With that confession, Jesus begins a teaching on Kingdom and the rebirth. In the translation we miss the subtle way in which the Lord was expressing Himself and, therefore, we also miss the importantance of Jesus' choice of words when He replied to Nicodemus' confession.

The word *born* in the Greek is *gennaō*, which is sometimes used of men begetting children. In the Old Testament the biblical genealogies also support this concept of the origin of birth. In the Old Testament the Hebrew word *yalad* is translated "beget," which means to father or to cause to exist. This Hebrew word is never used to describe a mother and the birth of a child. So "born," in the sense of "beget," is an activity of the father. The word *again* comes from another Greek word, *anōthen*, which means from above, again, or anew. So we would be correct to say that "born again" may mean to be begotten or caused to exist by the Father from above.

The word *kingdom* is *basileia* in Greek. It means sovereignty, royal power, or the sphere of God's rule. When the earth is in rebellion against God, then His Kingdom is that sphere where, at any given time, His rule or reign is acknowledged. Daniel 2:44 says that God has established a kingdom that will never be destroyed and will not be left to people who are not familiar with Him. It will crush every kingdom that tries to rise against His and they will be brought to an end. The Kingdom of God will never end. It will endure forever.

In His words to Nicodeums, Jesus said that unless a person is begotten or caused to exist by the Father from above, he cannot see, perceive, or understand (have both knowledge of and insight into) God's eternal Kingdom. Furthermore, Jesus confirmed Nicodemus' assertion of Christ's ancestry and current relationship with the Father. Nicodemus maintained that what Jesus had done was indicative of an "other worldly" endowment. It implies that the Lord's origin comes from God, or to put it another way, He is begotten of the Father.

Nicodemus also maintained that the results of His actions were indicative of a communing, contemporary fellowship with the Father. According to Jesus, this activity, which produces miraculous signs and wonders, can only come from a Kingdom where the Father's rule and sovereignty are acknowledged. Nicodemus' understanding of Jesus' origin was elementary and crude. So, Jesus expanded the theme of His own existence. He used this opportunity to explain that the first step in comprehending His miracles is to be born or begotten of the Father.

The second is to recognize God's rule and authority. This orients the new born-again person to the Kingdom and offers the opportunity to walk in obedience to Kingdom principles. As the new creation perceives and understands the principles, he is cognizant of the fact that the Kingdom is the reservoir from which the divine feats originate. These are the same feats that Nicodemus had heard of Christ performing.

In John 3:4 Nicodemus revealed both his interest in and his reservation of this spiritual phenomenon. He asked, "How can a man be born when he is old?" Nicodemus is thinking in worldly terms and from this perspective rebirth is not possible. He confirms this thought with a second question, "Can a man enter the second time into his mother's womb, to be born?" Inherent in these two questions is the war between the flesh and the spirit. These two questions, though innocent and seemingly innocuous, represent the battle between the temporal and the eternal. They are indicative of the gulf that must be traversed when dealing with the whole notion of the second birth.

The flesh, in an effort to maintain control, raises flesh-related issues. The flesh demands attention and challenges any answer that would resolve the issue on spiritual terms. Christ's initial response, "You must be born again," shocked Nicodemus' natural understanding. Jesus was fully aware of Nicodemus' position in society and his family history. Jesus used this knowedge and caused him to deal with the inadequacy of all that he is, and of his rituals, position, temporal authority, and ancestry. Nicodemus was then faced with making a choice. If he stays where he is, though, he will never walk in the place where the divine majesty and power of Christ are operative.

Up to this encounter with the living Christ, everything Nicodemus knew only supported his disbelief of the divinity of Christ. So Jesus told Nicodemus that his comfortable Pharisaical past had to go if he was to ever understand and enter the true Kingdom of God.

Jesus saw no fault in Nicodemus' coming to Him by night. He knows that all who come to Him will face the choice of entering into a revolutionary and life-changing experience. Everything of the past will bring into question the power and reality of Christ. Family tradition will try to sway them from believing in the Son of the living God. In the end, to fully know Christ and to have fellowship and communion with Him will require each person who responds in the affirmative to Christ, to put the past aside.

A closer look at this war between the flesh and the spirit will help us understand the paradigm shift or the life-changing decisions required to experience the fullness of the second birth. We must not underestimate Nicodemus' questions because they are the mental springboard from which he made his initial approach to the Lord. As a Pharisee and devout Jew with a rich family history, he did not seek the Lord in a vacuum. He brought all that he is, his biological baggage, when he came by night to meet Jesus. He brought the family's idiosyncrasies and hidden secrets, his genetic dispostions, and the customs he has been taught. In his encounter with the Lord, he was saddled with religious ideology and traditions that span time and history. When he met Jesus in the dark, the slate of his life was not clean. It was loaded with earthly trappings.

Jesus, on the other hand, was not concerned with who Nicodemus was then. He was showing Nicodemus a paradigm shift that, if accepted, would cause Nicodemus to become something different from that time forward. In this new and different place, Nicodemus began to view birth and all that goes with it in a different light. Nicodemus' past burden is not unique to him alone, however. Each of us who approaches Jesus Christ does so with a closet full of family skeletons, a chest of family mysteries and unexplained phenomena, and a wealth of mental images and beliefs that are characteristic of and unique to our family.

Like Nicodemus, we approach the Lord with our preconceived notions of His person and His character. We pursue Him through the paradigm we have accepted as the basis for His identity. In the beginning, this is the only model we can use to understand Him. But we will never fully understand nor seriously consider the life and the word of Christ if we allow our natural thoughts to guide us in trying to understand Him.

> *Wherefore henceforth know no man after the flesh; yea though we have known Christ after the flesh, yet now henceforth know we* Him *no more* (2 Corinthians 5:16).

For us, knowing Christ after the flesh means establishing a knowledge of Him based upon our fleshly response to

Him. But such knowledge is limited in its scope and causes us to fall short in our relationship with Christ. We live and function far below the original intent of the Father.

If we embrace every facet of the new birth, we can trade our collection from our family heritage, both positive and negative, for a spiritual inheritance in God's true Kingdom. We can swap the first order, which is insufficient and ineffectual, for the second order, which is more than sufficient. The first order is life in the staus quo, but the second order produces a life-changing beginning.

Hebrews 10:9 reminds us that the Lord takes away the first so He can establish the second. In the doctrine of rebirth, although it is not necessary to separate from one's family, it may direct less emphasis in that area. At the same time, it will cause us to place greater emphasis on our allegiance to our relationship with Jesus. Matthew 10:34-37 in the New King James Bible says this:

Do not think that I came to bring peace on earth. I did not come to bring peace but a sword. For I have come to "set a man against his father, a daughter against her mother, and a daughter-in-law against her mother-in-law"; and "a man's enemies will be those of his own household." He who loves father or mother more than Me is not worthy of Me. And he who loves son or daughter more than Me is not worthy of Me (Matthew 10:34-38 NKJ).

The second birth supersedes our first or biological birth. As a means of salvation, it delivers us from genetic disorders that make us dysfunctional and cause us to walk in the flesh. Actually, the second birth is our redemption. Through the sacrificial death of Jesus Christ, the price for our deliverance has been paid. All of the family curses and biological dysfunctions that plagued our ancestors and have threatened to render us and our seed submissive to their influence, have been satisfied. We have been set free to resist a return to the life of the flesh. We have been freed from the influence of the enemy, whose purpose is to render us ineffective and to lessen our contribution to and work for the Kingdom of God.

The enemy is delighted when we choose to hold on to the old paradigm that makes us victims and fosters low self-esteem. The old paradigm renders us powerless and promotes apprehension of spiritual things. It lulls us into complacency and encourages us to walk after the flesh rather than in the spirit. If we continue in the old way, we will offer excuses for our behavior as we blame our family background, culture, and tradition for the quality of our walk or the lack thereof. Certainly, Nicodemus is an excellent example of my point.

Thanks be to God! The second birth frees us from the trappings that hinder our walk with Him. It causes us to know that, despite the biological facts of our lives, there is a way to go beyond the confines of the flesh.

And as we have borne the image of the earthy, we shall also bear the image of the heavenly (1 Corinthians 15:49).

In a verse prior to this one the apostle Paul writes,

Howbeit that was not first which is spiritual but that which is natural; and afterward that which is spiritual (1 Corinthians 15:46).

Notice carefully the order of occurrence. The first is natural. This means, in the beginning, we have no choice except to operate in the realm of the natural. All that we know or have capacity for is known to us in this arena. In the beginning, our thinking patterns, our reasoning and our behavior all flow from the natural paradigm. This, it would seem, is the course the Lord has established. By walking first in the natural, we can see the stark difference when we begin to walk in the Spirit. Also, with that second walk comes a bonus that was not possible with the first: we can see and enter the Kingdom of God. I believe we have scriptural evidence to confirm this.

And the Lord God formed man of the dust of the ground, and breathed into his nostrils the breath of life; and man became a living soul (Genesis 2:7).

Several issues are raised here. First, you will note that God formed the man. Genesis 1:27 says this:

So God created man in His own image, in the image of God created He him; male and female created He them (Genesis 1:27).

There is no question about the origin of man. We were created by the Father and designed in His image. Man's creation, through the use of natural elements, made the image of the Father visible. Then God breathed into the nostril He had formed from the dust of the ground. His breath, His Spirit, His life, filled the newly formed shape and man became a living soul. The form of man was not alive until he was filled with God's life-giving breath. The form of man was not spiritual even though God had formed him by His divine design and in His own image. It was not until God's breath had intercourse with the natural form of man that man became a spiritual living soul.

The act of creation was a paradigm shift. Man shifted from a dead form to a living substance, a spiritual soul. Suffice it to say, the natural man is only the first stage of a process because this natural, living substance is subject to death. Romans 8:6 says this:

For to be carnally minded is death... (Romans 8:6).

However, God's plan was for man to continue to live after the body had passed away. The first order or stage was not the destination of man. This explains Second Peter 3:9 which says:

The Lord is not slack concerning His promise, as some men count slackness; but is longsuffering to us-ward not willing that any should perish, but that all should come to repentance (2 Peter 3:9).

The Lord does not desire for us to remain submitted to the first order of existence, which leads to death. This explains why, from the very beginning, He devised the intercourse of His Spirit with natural man so His creation could move into the second order—the spiritual life. Now we can understand Romans 8:6, which says, "...to be spiritually minded is life and peace." We have not begun to experience a life filled with God's peace if we have not accepted the second birth that has been provided for us in the realm of the Spirit.

In one final example, the life of the apostle Paul supports the notion that the second order replaces the first. In Philippians 3:3, when Paul admonishes the people to have no confidence in the flesh, he also quickly admits that if such confidence were warranted, he would be a prime candidate to rest upon fleshly laurels. Verses 4-6 say this:

> *Though I might also have confidence in the flesh. If any other man thinketh that he hath whereof he might trust in the flesh, I more: circumcised the eighth day, of the stock of Israel, of the tribe of Benjamin, an Hebrew of the Hebrews; as touching the law, a Pharisee; concerning zeal, persecuting the church; touching the righteousness which is in the law, blameless* (Philippians 3:4-6).

Notice Paul's list of his past. He was born a Jew of the tribe of Benjamin. He called himself a Hebrew of Hebrews. He was a Pharisee and with great zeal he persecuted the Church and walked blamelessly in keeping the ordinances and statutes of the law. He, like all of us, has a past filled with fleshly baggage. But there was a paradigm shift offered to him. Verse 7 points out the effects of this paradigm shift when Paul's first life was made null and void.

> *But what things were gain to me, those I counted loss for Christ* (Philippians 3:7).

All of this past baggage Paul considered, in one moment, to be loss. It was not a process of losing. He proclaimed his first order of life as one loss, which occurred once and for all. But, although the loss is once and for all, the implementation of the second order is a process. Paul admits that he must die daily as he proceeds further into his walk with God. Therefore, this paradigm shift changed Paul's life so radically that he was actually transformed. Verses 8-14 outline what he gained through this second birth. Paul says that this paradigm shift, which caused him to denounce his biological birth and all its trappings, opened him up to receive the following:

- the excellency of his knowledge of Christ Jesus,

- the recognition of Jesus Christ as Lord,

- the proper perspective of his having gained fellowship with Christ, and

- his being clothed in the righteousness of Christ as opposed to his own fallible righteousness.

It is important that we understand that this paradigm shift was radical. It was so radical that it affected every facet of Paul's existence. His mind, the essence of his soul, and of course, his spirit, were not merely challenged. They were changed when he was freed from the strangle hold of his former life. His obedience to the call of God enabled him to walk in the Spirit instead of in the flesh. With this understanding of the war between the spirit and the flesh, we can better understand and consider Nicodemus' visit to Jesus Christ.

Included in Nicodemus' words are the following ideas or questions:

1. Is this a physical anomaly? Birth is a physical puzzle and, physiologically, rebirth seems to be impossible.

2. Doesn't rebirth fly into the face of physiology, biology, and genetics?

3. Does being born again have anything to do with starting life all over again?

4. What does this concept do to the earthly family and the genetic and inculcated traditions inherent in being in a biological family?

All of these questions find their basis in and originate from the wisdom of man. They represent the very best thinking of the carnal mind. They follow the contours of thought that reflect the accepted wisdom and culture of life in worldly terms. We ought not be surprised by these earthbound questions. Paul recognized the manifestation of this kind of thinking in the church at Corinth. In First Corinthians 2:11-14, he wrote the following to the people in the Corinthian church:

For what man knoweth the things of a man, save the spirit of man which is in him? even so the things of God knoweth no man, but the Spirit of God. Now we have received, not the spirit of the world, but the spirit which is of God; that we might know the things that are freely given to us of God. Which things also we speak, not in the words which man's wisdom teacheth, but which the

Holy Ghost teacheth; comparing spiritual things with spiritual. But the natural man receiveth not the things of the Spirit of God: for they are foolishness unto him: neither can he know them because they are spiritually discerned (1 Corinthians 2:11-14).

Undoubtedly, we have all asked these kinds of questions regarding the process of being born again. We, like the people in the Corinthian church, come into the second birth from a base of operation located within the earthly realm. Because the rebirth is a spiritual phenomenon, the natural mind is unable to comprehend the concept. To fully comprehend the idea of the second birth, we must release our spirit to mingle with the Spirit of God. Then we will be taught by the Spirit of God and in His teaching He will reveal the whole truth to us. As we examine the life of our Lord Jesus Christ, His relationship with the flesh and the spirit will be a beacon to light the way for our spirits to understand the depths of His teachings.

And so it was, that, while they were there, the days were accomplished that she should be delivered. And she brought forth her firstborn son, and wrapped Him in swaddling clothes, and laid Him in a manager; because there was no room for them in the inn (Luke 2:6-7).

It is important to note that Mary *brought forth* her firstborn son, Jesus. The New Testament never says that Jesus was begotten of Mary. Matthew 1:16 says this:

And Jacob begat Joseph the husband of Mary, of whom was born Jesus, who is called Christ (Matthew 1:16).

Luke 3:23 then says this:

And Jesus Himself began to be about thirty years of age, being (as was supposed) the son of Joseph, which was the son of Heli (Luke 3:23).

In the Greek, another word for "born" is *tiktō*, which means to bear or bring forth as a mother births a child, or to produce from seed as the earth produces plants. The mother is the vessel through which the child is born, but first she must receive a seed to begin the process that ends with birth. *Tiktō* speaks of the final stages of the physiological process, the phenomenon of delivering the child. Matthew 1:21 uses the word *tiktō* to describe the way Mary will give birth to Jesus. However, this Greek word is not used when the supernatural birth of Jesus Christ is discussed. A form of the word *gennaō* is used instead. Like Jesus Christ, each of us has experienced *tiktō*, but if we are to seek the Kingdom and understand the Kingdom, we must also experience a spiritual *gennaō*, which is to be begotten of the Father from above. We must fully understand that, when we are born again, begotten of the Father, He no longer allows the years of abuse, family dysfunction, and religious tradition to define Jesus Christ and His Kingdom. Our second birth brings an end to everything we have inherited from the past that is foreign to our heavenly Father. We are free from any and all family curses and inheritances that flow to us from the flawed estate of our earthly family. Through Jesus Christ, we are free! We are free to ask, "How does it work?"

Chapter 4

A Moment in Time

Although the second birth experience is only one moment in the expanse of time, the results of that moment have an eternal effect on a person's life. When someone is born again, that person releases his or her fleeting life in the temporal world and tenaciously possesses the divine rewards of life in the eternal Kingdom of God. It is awesome to suddenly realize that Almighty God, the God of the universe, accepts our conscious decision to set aside the flesh to submit to His Spirit. Then, our awe of this moment turns to peaceful comfort as our spirits respond to the call of His Spirit and we are removed from the restrictions of the earthly and the ordinary. The second birth opens to us the vistas of the larger life, a vast world known as the spiritual realm, a realm full of frontiers to be conquered and enjoyed.

Even though this experience is quite real, it is also "other-worldly." On the other hand, there is a more practical result of the rebirth. In that moment of time, we are changed. We actually become different people. Too often we get caught up in the external at the very moment the internal is being reborn. The process of being born again has absolutely nothing to do with an outward display, such as an altar call. The second birth takes place in the intimacy of the spirit. Once the spirit has been reborn, it takes charge, complete charge, of the newborn's life. This reborn spirit witnesses with the Spirit who empowered it and, through this radical change, the born-again person's life is guided to function and cooperate with the Holy Spirit.

Without radical change, without a drastic shift from the old traditional paradigm to the new, born-again paradigm, there is no rebirth. Without the rebirth, the effort to be righteous, effort that is supported by religious emotions, produces only temporary results. These efforts are temporary because the people lack the power to live as born-again believers. There is no power in the first order of birth because the spiritual genetic patterns were never passed on. The seed of spiritual rebirth was missing because there was no intercourse. Without intercourse there is no spiritual copulation, and thus no birth. The first order of birth lacked that intense intimacy when the spirit of man, with eager anticipation, welcomed this spiritual intercourse with the Spirit of God. Without the power of the Spirit, the result is empty platitudes, false promises, short-lived prohibitions, legalism, and frigid encounters with others. Eventually this leads to death. The letter of the law, without the Spirit of God, kills, but the Spirit brings life (see 2 Cor. 3:6).

The new birth is spiritually painless because Jesus Christ went through the travail and the agony of childbirth on the cross of Calvary. The bleeding, the suffering, the pain, and the anguish were required if future sons and daughters of the Father were to be born. Notice, though, that we were born of the Spirit and not brought forth by the Spirit. Had we been merely brought forth, then our second birth would have been tainted with the stain of the flesh and carnality, which are the precise burdens from which we desire to be delivered.

In essence, during that miraculous moment in time, we died to the old life and were resurrected into the new life. We were born anew by the power of the same Spirit who raised Jesus Christ from the dead. Although the Spirit of God is pure spirit, He can move and operate in the human realm. Filled with His power, we are now able to deal with the human arena in a totally different way. Born-again people are new creations. Those who have been born again encounter the hand of God and are remolded to enjoy a new life, never again to be the same as they were before.

Ezekiel 16 speaks of God's hand being upon Israel. In this chapter the prophet Ezekiel chronicles the plight of God's people. Many of us can identify with the problems faced by these people because they reflect issues similar to those we have experienced. The first part of this chapter points out the dysfunction associated with biological birth, the first birth. It examines the detestable practices of God's people and outlines their aberrant, ungodly behavior. The prophet describes the people's birth in the land of the Canaanites, where their father was an Amorite and their mother a Hittite. These nations were the enemies of God's people. Ezekiel is revealing a view of God's people who were born in a system that is the exact opposite of the life style He had ordained for His people. As products of this corrupt system, they were genetically programmed with the ideals and fundamentals of that system. In the incubator of this society, the culture and the patterns of behavior that characterized the Canaanites, the Amorites, and the Hittites were passed on to the people of God. In verse 4 Ezekiel explains this:

> *On the day you were born your cord was not cut, nor were you washed with water to make you clean, nor were you rubbed with salt or wrapped in cloths* (Ezekiel 16:4 NIV).

The prophet presents a list of post-natal abuses that initiated God's people into a life style far below His original intention. When a child is born, the first order of business is to cut the umbilical cord. Once cut, the newborn must be in a position to receive nourishment outside the mother's womb. In the system described by Ezekiel, the people had no opportunity to receive God's nourishment. They are caught in the womb of a foreign culture and they are being fed only from the food provided by the Hittite mother. The child is constantly dependent upon the mother, who is herself feeding on a cultural smorgasbord that God never intended to feed His children. This smorgasbord included the rituals and customs of the enemies of God. God's sons and daughters were not called to follow in these ways or to think these thoughts. His seed was never to partake of this anti-God culture.

The child's life was of no value and the parent was not concerned with the child's welfare because the Scripture says that the child was not washed, rubbed with salt, or wrapped in cloths. There was no nurturing, no caring for the child. This child was an object of abuse at the hands of the same system that brought it life. This child was brought forth, but not begotten. The child did not enjoy the benefits of compassion and unconditional love. Ezekiel 16:5 says that the child was thrown out into an open field. From the very day the child was born, she was despised.

The major concern of the world system is to birth multitudes of people who will move, adhere to, and promote its diabolical agenda. The world system delights in those who have become insensitive robots and whose sole purpose is to enhance the cultural capital it is accumulating. These people become cold and frigid advocates of the system and are relentless in propagating the doctrines of the world's system. It is imperative that we understand the position of the world's system on the value of human life. Human life is of no importance to the world unless it furthers the cause of the world order.

Ezekiel tells us that the child is fed from a distance, the length of the umbilical cord, and only by the mother. There is no touching, no intimacy, no nurturing, only the constant feeding on the mother's provision. It is a pitiful condition in which God's people find themselves. Cast away, abused, malnourished, left to grow wild rather than lovingly nurtured, they are seemingly without hope. The tenets of the world system, which are set up to protect the system, do not permit establishing and maintaining a loving, intimate relationship. To allow such a relationship would invalidate its goals and render the system ineffective. These same tenets minimize and demean the domain of relationship and community, while they emphasize individualism and exploitation. This helps maintain the status quo of the system.

The world system desires to destroy the people of God because these people are predestined to be conformed to the likeness of Jesus Christ. The people God calls His own are foreordained to become the firstborn among many brothers and sisters who will be members of the family of God. Until we grasp this fact, we will remain helplessly exposed to the contagious disease of the world's order. The people of God must come to grips with the fact that the enmity between themselves and the world is a force to be reckoned with as well as a present reality. First John 2:15 admonishes us:

Love not the world, neither the things that are in the world. If any man love the world, the love of the Father is not in him (1 John 2:15).

The Amplified Bible in verses 16 and 17 states this:

For all that is in the world, the lust of the flesh [craving for sensual gratification], and the lust of the eyes [greedy ongoings of the mind] and the pride of life [assurance in one's own resources or in the stability of earthly things]— these do not come from the Father but are from the world [itself]. And the world passes away and disappears, and with it the forbidden cravings (the passionate desires, the

*lust) of it; but he who does the will of God and carries
out His purposes in his life abides (remains) forever*
(1 John 2:16-17 AMP).

The first five verses of Ezekiel chapter 16 paint a hard,
seemingly hopeless picture. The child of God is seen as
the abused, effectively neglected offspring of the world
system. Is there no way out of this world of decay? Read
on, because in verse 6 a paradigm shift occurs.

In Ezekiel 16:6 the Lord passes by and sees the child
kicking about in her blood. At the very moment the life
forces are leaking out, when the condition of the child is
at its worst, the Lord enters and the child is surrounded
by His presence. While thrashing about in the blood of
her humanity, the divine presence of Almighty God
came to her, observed her condition, and spoke life back
into her body.

This is the response of a caring God to the conditions
of His people. At the point when all seems lost, when we
are wallowing in self-pity and physical discomfort and are
helpless to overcome the adversities, the King of Glory
passes by. He sees our plight and without hesitation He
acts to relieve our pain. But more than simply making us
comfortable where we are, He also offers us the chance
to change our very existence. Oh, that we might understand that the details and conditions of our humanity are
not fixed in eternity! We have not been sentenced to a
life of imprisonment in the jail of an uncaring world. We
are not condemned to experience over and over again
the bloodbaths of our abusive past. The God who passes
by delivers us and sets us free from the pains of our past.

His message is but one word: "Live!" It is a message so short and so clear that we cannot fail to hear and understand. With this one word, He breathes life into a defeated, malnourished, abused infant.

Does this seem impossible? Do the conditions of this child's post-natal existence seem too great for the God of the universe to change? The command to live must have been met with disbelief. The child felt anguished as she looked at the circumstances affecting the flesh and realized the impossible task of complying with the Lord's instructions. Every facet of her life was intolerable. The society in which she lived discounted her. She had no real intimacy with her mother. The Scriptures don't even mention her father, who may have abandoned her. She lives a life of desperation, the victim of circumstances created for her by an abusive parent. But, fear not, for the Lord passes by, sees her condition, and declares to her: "Live!"

Does this story seem familiar? I am sure it sounds familiar to many. Our pasts are filled with the effects of malfunctions in our genetic patterns. We have been used as pawns of a system that guarantees our ultimate defeat in the game of life. The circumstances of our lives reek of abandonment, pain, abuse, and disdain. No matter how we attempt to conceal our pain, the inner person, unschooled in the day-to-day process of renewal, is facing a tortuous death either by murder or by self-inflicted annihilation.

Even as adults, many still wallow in their own blood— the blood of familial iniquity, the blood of genetic dysfunction, the blood of family disease that continues to course through the veins of each successive generation. It is a curse! Self-help courses and psychological answers lack life-changing power. There simply aren't enough resources in either the secular or the religious institutions to begin to attack the heart of the malady.

The sickness is a contagious plague that seeks to drain the life of the afflicted and to compel its victims to walk in the leprosy of the world system. It is determined to orchestrate both our natural and spiritual death. It intends for us to maintain the "blood is thicker than water" attitude without fully understanding the spiritual significance of such a declaration. But in the midst of this real and depressing malaise, the Lord says, "Live!"

The words of Jesus in John 10:10 reverberate in my mind. Jesus said, "I have come that they may have life, and have it to the full" (NIV). I believe Jesus is saying, "I have come by and observed the conditions of your earthly existence. But, My coming has a specific purpose. I have not come by to merely observe your pitiful condition or to leave you without hope or help in the midst of your present circumstance. I have come by and measured your life with the measuring rod of life I have within Me and have concluded your life to be deficient and wanting. But neither have I come to merely pronounce judgment upon your condition. I have come by to tell you to live! I have come so you might have life and that more abundantly. I have come to remove the stigma and to forgive the iniquity you embraced as a pawn of the world of the flesh. A new order and a new paradigm I am offering to those who up till now simply existed, bound by the status quo. I have come to offer life—a life so new that it defies the laws of natural birth. It propels you into the heavenly realm and unlocks the mysteries of the new creation, a divine dimension that is unapproachable through the paradigm of the flesh. I pronounce death to the realm or paradigm of flesh. I pronounce life to you even while your present set of circumstances, reeking of impending doom, destruction, and death, prophesy pain and unrelenting distress. But, I say, *LIVE!*"

The answer to the child who is struggling to believe in the impossible is offered in Ezekiel 16:7. It is the Lord who will provide the power. It is the Lord who will make the way. It is the Lord who will make provision for this new life He has commanded. In this verse the words of the Lord are:

I have caused thee to multiply as the bud of the field and thou hast increased and waxen great, and thou art come to excellent ornaments: thy breasts are fashioned, and thine hair is grown, whereas thou wast naked and bare (Ezekiel 16:7).

The New King James Version renders it this way:

I made you thrive like a plant in the field; and you grew, matured, and became very beautiful. Your breasts were formed, your hair grew, but you were naked and bare (Ezekiel 16:7 NKJ).

The key to this miraculous paradigm shift was the presence of the Lord. By His own hand, He intervened and changed the natural order. There was no earthly mechanism that could bring about the transformation of this malnourished and mistreated child. Only the intervention of the hand of God could have brought about such a metamorphosis. Now is the time to understand that our struggle to be free from the constraints of our past, and the pains that go along with that struggle, will only be accomplished when it is accompanied by the sovereign hand of Almighty God. There is no other solution to such a dilemma. The predicaments and the conditions of our humanity present an opportunity for God to dispense His divine power on our behalf, so His original intent, once and for all, will be accomplished.

There is another important point that must be understood. This life-changing shift was a radical change for this child. It was a change that was completely unexpected and unpredictable, given the tenor of the living conditions of the child. You may ask, "How could this child be turned into so beautiful a person, given the set of circumstances in which she was born?" We have been entertained by the Horatio Alger epics that tell of persons picking themselves up by their bootstraps and we are aware of the Pygmalion effect on the lives of people, but neither of these can adequately explain the hand of God moving in the life of an individual. No earthbound story can compare to the radical change that occurs when a person sheds the old and becomes brand-new.

In the world system, it is the new that turns old. But in the economy of God, He reverses the sequence and makes the old become new again. Better yet, when God is the force behind the change, the new becomes better than the original. The old is tarnished with the darkness of the flesh; the new shines with the light of the divine. The old is temporal and confines the individual in the quicksand of the carnal realm; the new is located in eternity. The old imprisons; the new liberates. The old is cursed; the new is blessed. The old is deadening; the new is quickening.

Oh, that we would fully understand the liberating power of the second birth. It is the highest demonstration of the Father's grace and mercy. The second birth changes a person from a victim to a liberated Christian, one free from natural anxiety and worldly fear. It empowers us to rise above the limitations of the earthly realm. The second birth makes us impervious to the intended pain and distresses the enemy intends for us. When we are brought forth from our mother's womb and not aborted, we experience a demonstration of God's grace. Then, when we are saved and are no longer the victims of the enemy's plans and schemes, the scales fall from our eyes and we can see clearly the wonderfully powerful results of our new birth.

Chapter 5

Transformed
to a New Realm

The Greek word for "new" is *kainos*, which denotes that which is unheard of or unused, not new in time, but new as to form or quality. It means to be of a different nature. This is the whole point of the second birth. It is often uncomfortable at first, as it catapults us into an unfamiliar realm filled with new challenges. The transformation is literal as we move from one kingdom into another. I would be seriously remiss if I failed to properly emphasize this kingdom transfer. The process of transformation introduces us to a totally different paradigm, a distinctly different mind-set, and a quality of life that was not even remotely possible in the kingdom of the flesh.

The quality of life is new. It is radically different from the "unborn-again" life style. I suggest that, while this change is spiritual, the manifestation of the second birth is in the realm of the soul and the flesh. If this were not the case, then the second birth would be merely a concept or an intellectual delicacy that is carefully examined and gingerly handled, but never eaten or digested. If the response is not valid, then the intended result of the transformation, which is a radically different life style, would not occur.

Concerning this whole concept of being born again, I believe we currently deal only with the ceremonial. We accept only the ritual associated with the second birth. We say the words of repentance, undergo water baptism and profess a newfound faith in Jesus Christ. But, are our life styles changed? Or do we confine the Spirit of God to the ethereal and continue life's journey with an unsanctified mind and body? Our spirits have had intimacy with God's Spirit, but the new child gets aborted by an uncircumcised heart and mind. This abortion interferes with God's plan, or ordained destiny, for our lives. We have a sanctified spirit, but the rest of us has yet to walk in that newness.

Paul helps us to understand the process of transformation in his letter to the Romans.

> *I appeal to you therefore, brethren, and beg of you in view of [all] mercies of God, to make a decisive dedication of your bodies—presenting all your members and faculties—as a living sacrifice, holy (devoted, consecrated) and well pleasing to God, which is your reasonable (rational, intelligent) service and spiritual worship. Do not be conformed to this world—this age,*

fashioned after and adapted to its external, superficial customs. But be transformed (changed) by the [entire] renewal of your mind—by its new ideals and its new attitude—so that you may prove [for yourselves] what is the good and acceptable and perfect will of God, even the thing which is good and acceptable and perfect [in His sight for you] (Romans 12:1-2 AMP).

This is as powerful revelation of the way in which every part cooperates in the process of transformation. It is the body that is offered as a living sacrifice. In order to be fit or acceptable, the body must first be sanctified—completely set apart for service to God. At the same time, the mind must be renewed.

Something takes place in the realm of the soul that works in cooperation with the spirit and the flesh. At the time of salvation, our spirits acknowledge our position in the Lord. However, this is only the beginning of the process. Once our spirits put us into position, we must prepare to present our bodies and all of the body's members for the renewing of the mind. If we are to truly see the born-again life style manifested on the earth, then we must take seriously and embrace the command to renew our minds.

The word "renew" in Greek is *anakainō*. *Ana* is a prefix that means back or again and *kaino* means new; not recent, but different. The use of this word is important because it emphasizes the whole idea of our minds being new *again*. In Ephesians 4:23, Paul admonishes the people in the church at Ephesus to be renewed in the spirit of their minds. It is no coincidence that Paul links the spirit and mind because the renewal of the mind, or the mind being different *again,* is a vital point. Within this concept is an understanding that the second birth is a work performed only by the Holy Spirit.

Perhaps you are thinking, "Was the mind different when it was new the first time?" Since our minds are to be renewed or made new again, it seems logical to assume there was a time in the past when they were new. Were the thoughts of our minds in the past completely opposite to the thoughts of our minds prior to our being born again? If the renewal of our minds through the second birth is the second time our thought processes have been changed, then at what point in the past were our thoughts just like our renewed, born-again thoughts are now?

Before we explore the answer to this question, it is vitally important that we understand that the renewed mind is the key to walking in the fullness of the second birth. Through a sanctified mind, a mind that has become the mind of Christ, we are able to follow the instructions of the sanctified spirit. It is these instructions that are essential for the body to walk in the newness of life. That is the key. That is the synergism that is necessary if we are to walk free of the "pre-born-again" life style and in agreement with the life style of the second birth. The spirit, soul, and body all respond to the sanctification that results from our being born again. But, it is our spirits that work to conform our souls and bodies and align them with the spiritual inheritance of our second birth. The Holy Spirit witnesses with our spirits that we are, positionally, the sons and daughters of God. Through the anointing of the Word of God, our souls are filled with the reality of who we really are through the atoning death of Jesus Christ. We are positively changed by accepting, through faith, all the promises of a life in the spirit realm.

So, the spirit prods the soul and the body to get in step spiritually. Our spirits constantly proclaim to our souls and our bodies the excellent benefits and the importance of lining up with the will and the purpose of God. At times we are aware of the cooperation between the trinity of self as each part works in unison. When all three are in agreement, we stand in a place of spiritual equilibrium. We are seated with Jesus Christ in heavenly places, utilizing every spiritual gift in a life of abundant joy.

The Most Holy Place, the realm of pure spirit, calls us to enter wholeheartedly and without reservation into the arena of the Father, the Son, and the Holy Ghost. It is here that we can live out our lives filled with the blessings of the second birth. In the Most Holy Place everything is all God. There is no mixture, no variableness. It is the divine place filled with God's majesty, dominion, and power. We are challenged by a call to leave behind the flesh of the Outer Court—the ordinances of baptisms, the fundamentals of religious instruction—and to flow with the Spirit into the Holy Place, the place where spirit and soul become co-laborers. We are enticed by the purity of God's grace to go further into the Most Holy Place where we are absolutely consumed by the power and presence of God. It is the habitation of God, and He is with us. In this place there is a clear manifestation of Emmanuel. With a sweet taste in our mouth and the fragrant aroma of holiness in our nostrils, we long to rid our bodies and souls of anything that would hinder or impede our entering into the Most Holy Place, the Holy of Holies.

Praise be to God, the way of our entrance has been made secure through the unselfish act of Jesus Christ. He is our way, our truth, and our life. We cannot come to the Father in the Most Holy Place unless we come there through the agency of Jesus Christ. The mind must be renewed to see that this entrance is possible. The mind must return to where it once was. It must return to that time of intimacy with the Father—that time when everything was all God when the mind's only knowledge was the presence of the Father. This is the time when we had the mind of Christ the *first time*.

But when was this time? In what glorious era were our minds filled only with thoughts of God? Was there really a time when our quest for knowledge boiled down to knowing God and nothing else? When was that time when our tripartite nature was in perfect alignment with the triune Godhead? When did we last meditate on the ways of God and consider the works of His hands?

To find such a time, we must return to the place where God ventured into spatial reality. It was here that

He spoke and formed the fullness of the universe, the heavens and the earth and all that is in them. This was the time He first reached into the dust of the earth, made an image of Himself, and caused it to become flesh. This was the time He breathed into His fleshly image and His creation became a living soul. In the garden, the Spirit of God filled the mind of man. The division of spirit, soul, and body was not as evident as it is now. Man thought with the Spirit of his Creator. He acted upon the impulse of his spirit. He communed breath to Breath, spirit to Spirit, in a continual fellowship of agape and mutual respect. Man at this time had the mind of Christ for the very *first time*.

Preposterous, you say! Yet John's Gospel tells us, "In the beginning was the Word and the Word was with God, and the Word was God. The same was in the beginning with God" (Jn. 1:1-2). Since the Word became flesh and dwelt among us as the only begotten of the Father, then, before His transformation into the flesh, Christ was with the Father. Nothing that was made, was made without Him (see Jn 1:3). So when God breathed Himself into man, He also formed the spirit of man's mind for the first time. Since Christ was a part of God during this process of creation, then the mind of that first man was the mind of Christ. Adam's mind had to be the mind of Christ because the triune Godhead collaborated on the design and execution of the beloved creation. Man was destined to think as Christ. The Spirit of the living God had taken up residence in man's temple. Every thought of man originated from the mind of God. Man was privy to the secrets of God's knowledge and wisdom because He shared them through His intimate love with His creation.

Look at the similarities between the first and the last Adam. The first Adam was a creation of the Father and, as such, was content to know only God. He was in a blessed state, ignorant of doing evil or the ways of evil. The thoughts of the first man were steadfastly on his relationship with the Father and on carrying out His will and purpose for his life. His mind was void of any resource that would cause him to consider evil. His mental faculties were at peace and aberrant thoughts did not enter the process.

In the garden, man was consumed by God's love and enjoyed the awesome presence of God. His solitary purpose was to be the physical manifestation of the Father. His fellowship was only with God, so He was in the spirit at all times. He was in a position of complete, unquestioned obedience to the Father. For the first Adam, there was no question of personal opinions or alternative solutions. His thoughts were God's thoughts and he was content to be and do what God ordained. He had no personal objectives; a personal agenda was unthinkable. There was no notion or concept of human arrogance because man knew nothing more than God. There was no question of his being content and satisfied with this arrangement, for he knew nothing of discontent. The God he knew was more than enough.

The last Adam, Jesus, was the same as the first. Jesus Christ, as the first begotten son of the Father, was full of grace and truth. At His baptism, His spiritual heritage was proclaimed and confirmed from the heavens. It was the Father who spoke, as Second Peter 1:17 says, "...there came such a voice to Him from the excellent glory, This is My beloved Son, in whom I am well pleased." As with the first Adam, who had dominion and ruled over his place of habitation, the last Adam, Jesus Christ, has been given a kingdom by His Father. It is into this kingdom (see Col. 1:13) we, as believers, have been translated.

As the first Adam was in complete obedience to the Father, so is Christ in obedience. In John 5:19 Jesus says that the Son can do nothing of Himself. He only does what He sees the Father do. Jesus also says that the judgments He makes are based upon conversations with the Father (see Jn. 5:30). He does not seek His own will, but the will of His Father who sent Him. The last Adam, like the first, is content to express His oneness with the Father. It is out of this contentment that Jesus announces, "I and the Father are one" (Jn. 10:30 NIV).

Jesus' sole purpose and intent—to hear the Father's voice and to obey His commands—is stated in several places throughout the New Testament. It would be well for us to note that Adam and Christ were focused upon their mission. The lives of both were joined to and in communion with the Father. God's thoughts were their thoughts, His ways were their ways. They could be identified by their association with God. Their very natures, their characters, and their actions were directed, confirmed, and established by their fellowship with God. They existed in perfect communion with the Father and this communion defined their earthly roles.

The mind of Adam was the mind of Christ. He thought God's thoughts, reacted to God's desires, and was cultivated by the richness of their communion. This communion was so intense that the mind of God, the mind of Christ, and the mind of Adam were as one. In this state only spiritual thoughts occupy the cerebral activity of man. That is the mind of Adam and Christ. His mind, conformed to Christ, was the following:

- consumed with oneness with the Father,

- saturated with God's purpose,

- established upon obedience to the will of God,

- occupied with replicating what he had seen the Father do,

- built upon a constant communion and intimate fellowship with the Father, and

- submitted to the musings of God so distracting thoughts were eliminated.

That is the condition of the renewed mind. It is a mind absolutely consumed with being in oneness with the Father and focused upon fulfilling God's purpose. It is a mind established upon unconditional obedience to the will of God. This mind is a return to man's first mind. It is a mind predisposed to think only as God thinks. It is a mind that has no clue as to the concept of evil; a mind not distracted by second opinions or alternative ideas. This same mind must be the mind of the born-again believer. That is how the born-again life style functions. It is the result of a mind that has been sanctified by the Spirit of the living God and has returned to its former condition before the fall of man.

Philippians 2:5-9 describes the mind of a believer who has taken on the mind of Christ. Examine this Scripture carefully and you will see what attitude this type of mind produces:

- Though being in the form of God, He made Himself of no reputation.

- He took upon Himself the form of a servant.

- He was made in the likeness of man.

- He humbled Himself and became obedient to death, even the death of the cross.

The mind of the born-again believer is susceptible to the notions of death and resurrection, as was Christ. There is no rebirth without death. Resurrection can only follow a demise. So in the born-again mentality, the mind of Christ is housed in a fleshly tabernacle. This tabernacle knows it was born in the image of God, and it is willing to let any thought of reputation die.

When we walk in the Spirit, the world's dominance over us decreases and the material things of the world— the perks and enticements that tickle the ego—are counted as nothing more than dung. If earthly treasures are offered as an enticement to compromise the cause of Christ, we reject the temptation. It is more than estrangement from the philosophical doctrines and dogmas of the world order. It is complete separation. It is a final divorce! Therefore, the lure of worldly things, including the offer of worldly esteem, is without value and substance. Such carnal trappings are not worthy to be compared to the glory of walking in heavenly places with Jesus Christ. The born-again mind has already traveled in the worldly paradigm. It has considered the many ideologies and worldly views that serve as the standard for thinking in the world order. An encounter with the Son of God, Jesus Christ, the risen Lord, causes that depository of worldly ideas and theories to be revealed as false promises. Ultimately, they are discarded as worthless distractions by the born-again believer.

It is impossible to overestimate the power of salvation. Our finite minds are incapable of comprehending the radical change in store for those who will take seriously their belief in Jesus Christ as the living Son of God. For those who do take it seriously, everything is different. Nothing can, or will, remain the same. We have left the old order, or the old world, and we have entered a higher realm. It is more than another dimension. It is a completely different way of thinking, founded on a totally different body of knowledge. Any description we place on this transformation will fall short of reality. It is, in fact, a literal translation from one kingdom to another.

Don't confuse it with mere church membership. It is not regular attendance at a worship service, giving alms, or doing good works. Don't confuse it with philanthropic activities or participation in causes that are established to better the plight of society's downtrodden. It is more than any of these mundane activities. The motivation that comes from the mind of Christ precedes activity and becomes the very foundation of the principles that produce regular attendance, tithing, good works, and even social betterment. In the moment it takes to complete the transfer to the Kingdom of God, thoughts are reordered to conform to Christ's thoughts. I don't mean mere philosophical assent and acceptance, but a radical elimination of one mind-set, and the tenacious possession of a new one, which revolutionizes one's entire life.

When I visualize this transfer, I see people actually leaving their physical residence and stepping into an eternal home. It is not the *Twilight Zone,* but it might easily be called the *Divine* Zone. In this realm, God's presence is in residence.

Man has created a God who is safe for human consumption, a watered-down version of His nature, so don't confuse the picture the world painted with what I am describing. I am not talking about casual encounters, but a constant presence. We can actually enter God's arena without the interferences of worldly paradigms or earthbound thinking. We can transcend the parameters of carnality and assume our blood-bought positions in the domain of God. This is the place where only the resurrected abide. Those who have died to self and the ways of the unrighteous, as well as to the thinking of this present world order, are free to enter. This is the place where those who were willingly crucified and then resurrected through Christ Jesus to new life, are positioned with Him in the Kingdom.

There is a sort of irony in being able to live with Him in His Kingdom, while we simultaneously continue an earthly form. More ironic is that the principles of this Kingdom create an earthly existence that is more tolerable. This is more than a change of physical location. This is the change of the fundamental issues of life.

Chapter 6

Understanding Your Position in the Kingdom

It is one thing to see the results of the second birth in the lives of others and quite another thing to enjoy the deeper walk with God for yourself. When Jesus confronted Nicodemus with the statement, "Except a man be born again, he cannot see the kingdom of God" (Jn. 3:3), He was trying to open Nicodemus' spirital eyes. Jesus wanted Nicodemus to understand the difference between the earthly kingdom that has Jewish tradition at the center and the Kingdom that places God in the center. John 1:12-13 will help us understand the concept of a divine-oriented Kingdom.

But as many as received Him, to them He gave the right to become children of God, to those who believe on His name: who were born, not of blood, nor of the will of the flesh, nor of the will of man, but of God (John 1:12-13 NKJ).

So those who are born of God are begotten of the Father and they are the only ones who can *see* the Kingdom of God. Without the mind of Christ, a gift made available through the rebirth, the existence of God's Kingdom is not evident. The word *see* in this context means to perceive or to understand. Jesus wanted Nicodemus to understand that, unless one is born again, he cannot fathom, understand, or even perceive the awesome notion of the Kingdom of God. Our natural, biological birth does not permit such insight. To gain this level of sight, God demands a second birth.

What about those who know about the Kingdom, but who haven't seen inside? They are bound by a religious spirit which has placed God in a traditional box. The mission of this type of spirit is supported by a leadership that spoon-feeds the established culture of "church" to a gullible membership. Perhaps they have avoided or clouded the issue by promoting teachings with titles like "Eschatology" or "The Theology of the End Times." In the end they allow this religious spirit to foil any attempt to break out of the snares of tradition and to seek the greater revelation of God. It is a trap to actually deflect the wondrous, unencumbered power of God that is available by understanding and accepting a place in the Kingdom.

The Church world, as a result, has weakened the link between the second birth and the understanding of the Kingdom. How many times have you heard a serious discussion of the second birth? The answer is, "Hardly ever." I would like to suggest a reason why the issue of the second birth is minimized: The process has been so watered down that the candidates see little or no difference between the new birth and life in the natural arena. The born-again experience has been reduced to a litany of do's and don'ts that touch nothing more than the outward behavior of mankind. Is it possible that the whole notion of the second birth lacks the dynamics that the Lord intended? With so much confusion and misinformation, is it any wonder that the genuine power of the second birth has remained a mystery to the religious community?

If the knowledge of being born again, and the resulting power of the Kingdom, was made known by the Church to its members, the entire foundation of the Church would first have to undergo a major paradigm shift. The myopic vision of the local church would have to be corrected. The nice but ineffective activities of the Church would have to be modified. The whole basis for worship and church attendance would undergo radical reconstruction and redefinition. Jesus says that being born again is the vehicle to understanding and being able to perceive the idea of the Kingdom of God.

It doesn't take a rebirth experience to understand the concept of church, but rebirth is absolutely necessary to understand the complexities of the Kingdom of God. Why? The Kingdom of God requires a constant expansion of understanding by its inhabitants. If these same inhabitants are part of a local church, their church will have to expand too. Such powerful change is not always met with enthusiasm by leaders and congregants who are determined to protect the status quo. Despite the work of an unbending leadership or of a religious spirit, who work to deny the power and existence of the Kingdom of God, God's Word reveals a Kingdom whose existence is everlasting. Daniel 2:44 says this:

And in the days of these kings shall the God of heaven set up a kingdom, which shall never be destroyed: and the kingdom shall not be left to other people, but it shall break in pieces and consume all these kingdoms, and it shall stand for ever (Daniel 2:44).

First Corinthians 4:20 says that the Kingdom of God is not in word, but in power. Romans 14:17 says that the Kingdom of God is not meat and drink, but righteousness, peace, and joy in the Holy Ghost. Luke 17:20-21 states that the Kingdom of God does not come with observation. People won't say, "See here" or "see there," for the Kingdom of God is within you. First Corinthians 15:50 tells us that flesh and blood cannot inherit the Kingdom of God; nor does corruption inherit incorruption.

These Scriptures represent a serious challenge to our traditional understanding of the Kingdom and its relationship to the individual believer. With the present system, we are hardly ever forced to face the truth. Nevertheless we must first understand that the Kingdom of God is an everlasting Kingdom that will never be destroyed. Proponents of tradition have used the issue of eschatology to establish limits on God's Kingdom.

The Kingdom of God will not cease to exist or fail to fully emerge simply because the best thinking of theologians cannot fathom the concept of an active, present-day Kingdom. God's eternal Kingdom exists beyond the confines of the conventional wisdom of scholars and theologians. God's Kingdom will not suffer demise simply because certain religious purists say so.

When the apostle Paul says that the Kingdom of God is in power and not in words, we should take note. The Greek word for "word" used in First Corinthians 4:20 is *logos*. It means intelligence or the expression of intelligence. *Logos* is regarded as the orderly linking or the connected arrangement of words in the inner thoughts. According to Paul, the Kingdom of God was not and is not developed from plans devised by or laid out as a result of man's intelligence. The Kingdom is not the brainchild of mental interaction. It did not suddenly appear; nor will it ever change through the mental reproductive process of man. It cannot be bound to the connected arrangement of words of the inward thoughts of man's mind or the feelings generated by emotional fantasies.

The Kingdom of God is of power, according to Paul. The word *power* in Greek is *dunamis. Dunamis* means inherent power. It stresses and implies ability or capability. The Kingdom of God does not rely on external forces. Instead it has the capacity to exist regardless of the condition of those who refuse to choose to live there. Whatever men think or object to regarding the Kingdom, it is complete in its own right. The kind of power inherent in God's Kingdom is perpetual. Unlike man-made power devices, it does not require recharging and it never runs down.

To the residents of the world, the power of the Kingdom is invisible power, causing the agenda of God to burst forth throughout the earth. The Kingdom and its inherent power reside within the disciples of Jesus Christ. There is no room for any other kingdom forces. At any given time, the kingdom of darkness cannot occupy the same position as the Kingdom of God, or the Kingdom of Light. Christians must reject any concept that does not promote the rule of God in their lives. God must reign surpremely. With God's rule apparent, the predestined purposes of God for your life will come to fruition.

Does this sound like traditional thinking? Does this sound like traditional "church" thinking? Do you see how different, how exceptional this concept of Kingdom is? Don't settle for a mind-set that is content to allow the status quo to remain intact rather than to allow the *dunamis* that lives within you to be manifested. The Lord had intended, from the very first day of man's creation, for His power to be evident. The Church must come to the stark realization that we, as a part of the Kingdom of God, are filled with the resident power of the Kingdom. We are empowered, capable, and filled with ability. We are designed, as Kingdom people, to see and enter the Kingdom and to function as instruments of the will of God. We are His soldiers and the mission He has planned cannot be thwarted by the enemy. We are to make sure that the Church assumes a true position of responsibility and that His plan is accomplished as He directs.

This brings us back to the necessity for the second birth. Jesus says that unless one is born again, the whole discussion of the Kingdom becomes moot. The element that fails in the natural, the spiritual renewal of the mind, is only available through the new birth. From a natural perspective we can understand and accept the traditional teachings and traditional ways. But this same fleshly, natural mind does not have the capacity to comprehend the things of the Spirit. The natural mind cannot understand even the most basic tenets, much less the complexities and intricacies of the Kingdom. Unless the natural has been abandoned for the spiritual; unless the first order has surrendered to the second; unless our natural, biological patterns have given way to spiritual patterns when we became born again, we will be forever imprisoned in a one-dimensional fellowship with God. Unless we reject every tradition that prevents our entrance into the Kingdom, we are doomed to take to our graves the dynamic, earth-shattering ideas and concepts of God.

God expects His design and plan, transferred to the mind of His creation, to be manifested on earth. Only our failure to live in the fullness of the second birth and our failure to apply ourselves to the Kingdom life style, will impede our destinies. We will never know the extent of God's incomparable power and majesty if we fail to comprehend these Kingdom concepts. The Church will remain set in its ways. It will continue to be a dead organization rather than a living organism. As long as we refuse to take our place, the agenda of the Church and the life of the Church will not flow in concert with the intentions of the Kingdom. We will be forever missing the mark, participating in innocuous, ineffective activities. We will be empty, lifeless, and powerless until we explore the truth of the Kingdom of God. Until we come to grips with the concept of God's Kingdom, we are destined to forever remain as a group of social clubs or social institutions. Ultimately, we will miss out on the power of God, the power He has reserved for those who have the spiritual insight to see the Kingdom of God. All is for naught, "Except a man be born again..." (Jn. 3:3).

The wisdom to use God's gift of power demands a newly-created mind. To fully comprehend the tenets of God's Kingdom, we must make a radical shift, a paradigm shift. This is a shift of enormous proportions. It is bigger than our local congregations. It encompasses an expanse that is unfathomable to the human mind. It is incomprehensible to the intellect of the unregenerate. The whole notion of God's Kingdom is anathema to those who are not walking by the Spirit. They are restricted to the confines of the natural realm and they have no fellowship with spiritual truths.

I want to restate a point I made earlier. It bears repeating. **There must be a total, radical reconstruction of the mind of the believer in order for the child of God to grasp the concept of the Kingdom.**

We may as well get prepared, if we are willing to take the plunge into the Kingdom, for it doesn't come peaceably. The born-again experience causes *chaos* in the life of the believer. There is no nice way to put it. When a person really becomes a new creation, his or her life must, spiritually and physically, go through a chaotic period.

In the life of the born-again believer, a time of reexamining issues and redefining beliefs occurs. All that a person holds sacred is reevaluated in light of the new birth.

Through this time of self-evaluation each person scrutinizes his or her life style. Every small facet of behavior is examined. The eye that used to examine each of these areas of one's life is no longer blocked by traditional lenses, which are out of focus. Instead, the eye is single and in focus. It is keenly aware of each imperfection. It has a greater depth of perception and it is able to weed out those actions that don't fit the example of the born-again life style. During this process, the normal life style is disrupted to such an extent that the person feels a loss of equilibrium. The status quo, in the past so firm and reliable, is destroyed as every facet of life is changed. The gauge for a geniune change from the natural to the spiritual, from the first birth to the second, includes the following:

- We question the validity of all the relationships we have and attempt to discover if they really glorify God.

- The basic structure of our day changes and we begin to schedule all that we do around our walk with the Lord.

- Our interests change radically.

- Our basic temperament changes, so much so that those who have been close to us can recognize the difference in us.

- Our interest in the spiritual realm, in walking with Jesus Christ, and in the pursuit of abiding in His presence becomes more important than our moving ahead in the natural realm.

- Our desire is to see others enjoy the same life-changing experience, and that desire moves us to find every possible way to tell others about the life of the born-again believer in Jesus Christ.

- We develop the essential disciplines for walking in the spiritual realm and, with tenacity and excellence, pursue their manifestation in our lives.

- With a longing heart, we seek for those times of quality fellowship and communion with the Lord, a time of spiritual intimacy and need, that no human is able to satisfy or fill.

I cannot stress stongly enough the way the genuine born-again experience changes everything about one's life. Thought patterns and the perceptions that once characterized our lives, are totally reconstructed to make room for the mind of Christ. When the chaos and disharmony propel us forward in the process of rebirth, every part of our lives is in opposition to the new life in the Lord Jesus Christ. The empowered spirit, once taken for granted or often dismissed as unnecessary, now causes us to abide in the presence of the Lord. We are as one who was dead and then gloriously alive. Individually, we go through a time of revival. We really are *resurrected.*

The resurrected spirit magnifies the chaos because it is not a part of the natural life style. Even the word *resurrection* is foreign to those who are caught by the trappings of the natural order and who lack any understanding of the realm of the Spirit or the Kingdom of God. Resurrection defies the laws of physical science. It does not compute in the biological systems of the world. The world of science accepts the concept of regeneration in the life of animals, and even in the life of man, but resurrection is considered too farfetched.

If biologists and scientists could see with their spiritual eyes, they would see the born-again life style is, in reality, an example of resurrection. Through the second birth, we have defied the laws of the natural realm by dying to every facet of life that is unlike God in any way. We actually die to the old life. We die to the old perspectives, the old ways of doing things, our old speech, our old behaviors, and our old iniquities. We undergo a death of the old person and, like Jesus Christ, we rise with newness of life. We are transferred from the kingdom of darkness into the Kingdom of God's dear Son. Hallelujah! That is why nothing remains the same. All things have become new. Old things have passed away. (See Second Corinthians 5:17.)

The force that accompanies such a transformation hurls the believer into a chaotic condition. This chaos is necessary. Out of the chaos comes order to the believer's life. This chaos is directed by the Lord. It is a necessary component of the resurrection. This chaos erupts, disrupts, overturns, and reorders. It abandons the old and releases fresh new systems into the life of the believer. It shuts down old life systems. It shatters. It shakes the very foundation of the former life style and thrusts us into a new Kingdom, the Kingdom of God.

The Lord told Jeremiah about this phenomonon. In Jeremiah 1:10 the Lord said "...to root out, and to pull down, and to destroy, and to throw down, to build, and to plant."

The principles used in the Kingdom of God create a positive effect when Kingdom residents use them. The person who has genuinely been born again finds himself operating in a totally different system. Our natural births and everything unique to that first birth are subordinate to the principles and the intentions of the second birth. No longer are we hostages to those family dysfunctions that characterize the natural birth. In the natural we limit ourselves with those sterotypical deficiencies. But when we are born again, none of the boundaries constructed by human endeavor and maintained by the spirit of narcissism can impede us. We are free to fulfill the purposes of God in our lives. In essence, the second birth relieves us from the strain of racial, social, and economic bias. The customs of the world system, designed to propagate the "chosen," are ineffective when applied to the born-again child of God.

As a part of our spiritual genetic make-up, we gain a resilience for overcoming. The weapons that were designed specifically to thwart us are useless. Our defense is spiritual, not carnal. To a world system intent on maintaining the status quo, the spiritual arsenal at our disposal is incomprehensible. As new creatures in Christ, we are no longer pawns of the prince of this world and we are not subject to his diabolical schemes. We walk with the authority of Jesus Christ, a gift from Him to Kingdom people.

This is where the whole issue of chaos is so important. When we are born again, the natural scheme of things, which is driven by a type of self-regeneration concocted by the world system's orchestration, is not able to control the outcome of our existence. We are out from under the sphere of influence propogated by the world system. Through our transformation, we are living by new rules, new dimensions, new hopes, and a new destiny. That time of chaotic change wreaks havoc on the established order. It disrupts the culture and ritual that formerly set the tone for our lives. The predisposition to submit to the dogma of the world system, planted in us during our natural birth, is null and void. We have seen the Kingdom of God and we are awed by its vastness and its splendor. Suddenly, we begin to perceive and comprehend the rule of God and we begin to believe it can become the guiding force for our lives. We begin to speak of Kingdom things with an understanding and confidence that come from a mind renewed in Christ. The dilemma, once hidden and then evident, is resolved at last!

Chapter 7

The Transcendent Nature of Kingdom People

When the second birth becomes a reality in the life of the believer, he or she receives a number of benefits. As the life of the believer begins to change, these benefits become evident. One of the many benefits of the second birth is a change in conditions. One such change is the shift in position of the believer from fixed to transcendent. The word *transcendent* refers to the spiritual luxury of reestablishing oneself in a totally new place. It is a place never before inhabited by the born-again believer. This transformation places the believer in a realm free of biological baggage. The past no longer dominates, influences, or determines the believer's future.

In Chapter 3, I dealt briefly with the subject of inherited or controlled behavior. Family members, particularly the older members, have a tendency to place constraints on anyone they can influence. They hope to control the actions and responses of those who will submit to their wills. It is only fair to state that godly training is important and much of what is passed on from generation to generation is sound advice. But there are many agendas in a family, some of which would be better off untaught. The problems associated with poor training are easily recognizable. Unfortunately, the person who has been trained improperly often continues to live under the influence of this training and is destined to repeat the same behavior over and over.

The same is true of social influences. To a greater or lesser degree, the peers of any age group wield a substantial amount of influence. Often people believe they must respond in a particular way if they are to achieve their goals and gain acceptance by the larger group.

These influences are but one of many issues that are nullified once a person experiences and walks in the light of the second birth. Poor or incorrect family values, social stigma, and improper goals lack potency in the life of the born-again believer. The mental and physical pressures, once in control of the person's life, no longer dominate or control the newborn believer. The believer is free from the ideas and examples that the world system places its stamp of approval on.

The biological heritage of those who have not been trained properly, does not provide the framework within which believers will find their destinies. The images that once plagued their minds and filled their thoughts have been rendered powerless. Concepts grounded in fantasy and mythology no longer emerge. Many families rely upon a form of family history and legend to create the incubator within which they weave their spells over the weaker family member. These traditions, which perpetuated the mystique of the family heritage, also established the family culture. Now, renewed in mind and spirit, filled with the mind of Christ, their backgrounds and their futures are not dependent solely upon the recordings found in the oral tradition.

Often family tradition has value and significance because it performs the function of moving the born-again believer to this place of transcendence. Once the believer accepts the shift, he is not concerned with trying to escape the past because it no longer has the impact or the influence it once possessed. The believer is free to make his own decisions and to allow Kingdom principles to become the guiding light of his destiny.

It is imperative that we understand the effect those issues or those circumstances, which have been such an integral part of our lives, have produced. They have caused us to fall prey to the "set up" the Lord has predestined for our lives. In Romans 8:28-29 the Amplified Bible says:

We are assured and know that [God being a partner in their labor], all things work together and are [fitting into a plan] for good to those who love God and are called according to [His] design and purpose. For those whom He foreknew—of whom He was aware and loved beforehand—He also destined from the beginning (foreordaining them) to be molded into the image of His Son

[and share inwardly His likeness], that He might be-
come the first-born among many brethren (Romans
8:28-29 AMP).

We who are now living for God and whose lives are
grounded in the call of God, are made sons of God. We
are actually being made to conform to the image of
God's Son, Jesus Christ. The born-again process added
fuel to the fire and released the power of God's original
plan.

This plan was for man to assume his place as the
product of His image. In the beginning, God was the
blueprint for man. The first man was to be the express
image of the Father on earth. Since God is a Spirit, man
would have to understand God through a spiritual intimacy if the progeny of the first man was to comprehend God. Man was to be the physical manifestation
of God, just as the Holy Spirit is the spiritual manifestation of God. In the flesh, man was to be a physical replica
of the Father. In the inner man, man's spirit was to be
the spiritual replica of God's Spirit.

God, in collaboration with the Son and the Holy
Ghost, designed and created the first Adam. The goal
was physical creation; the object of this goal was the
image of God. The fall of the first Adam disrupted God's
plan to relate to the earthly realm. To set His original
plan back in motion, God brought Jesus Christ into the
world.

And the Word [Christ] became flesh (human, incar-
nate) and tabernacled—fixed in His tent of flesh, lived

awhile–among us; and we [actually] saw His glory–His honor, His majesty; such glory as an only begotten son receives from his father, full of grace (favor, loving kindness) and truth (John 1:14 AMP).

Jesus Christ, as the second Adam and the manifestation of God's mercy and grace, succeeded where the first Adam failed. The first Adam's failure prevented the kind of intimacy God desired. So God the Father clothed Himself in humanity to provide an earthly model to serve as a pattern to which the newborn believer would be conformed. You should take note that God, in creating the second Adam, once again replicated or reproduced an image of Himself.

It is the design of God to multiply Himself through His creation by reproducing sons and daughters who conform to His image. Jesus is the express image of God and the second birth produces many brethren of Christ. These brethren are the multiplication of God's seed and are destined and designed to reflect God's image on the earth. It is often difficult, but essential to understand the awesome power of God where the second birth is concerned.

Yet to all who received Him, to those who believed in His name, He gave the right to become children of God–children born not of natural descent, nor of human decision or a husband's will, but born of God (John 1:12-13 NIV).

Under the reign of the second Adam, God's design was to give man the right to exercise his own free will in the process of becoming what he should have been. The decision to restore His relationship with man, as well as the process of replication, was the result of the deliberations of God. The second birth allows the original plan of God to be realized. It takes the particulars of the second birth and removes them from the realm of the natural. It makes them completely dependent upon spiritual principles and places the implementation of the restoration in the hand of the Spirit of God.

Although man submits his will to the requirements of God, he has no part in the process of transformation. Man cannot intervene in the process. Although man has an effect upon flesh-and-blood issues, the second birth is beyond his influence. The thinking of soulish man is incapable of designing or conceiving such a simple, yet powerful plan as the second birth. This is totally a spiritual enterprise. Sons and daughters are born to God because of God's will, not man's will. Those who became replicas of the prime object, the image of God, became the children of God through the will of God.

Flesh (earthly man) is discounted in the second birth experience. This initiates a life style that is grounded in the spirit realm, but an existence that is walked out in the natural. The dichotomy and the dilemmas resulting from such duality can be staggering if one is not absolutely certain of the issues involved in the born-again experience.

The renewed mind, characterized as the mind of the first Adam before his fall, constantly implores the believer to remember the liberty that has been purchased for him through the death of Jesus Christ. The renewed mind urges the believer to recognize that Jesus was his substitute in the death and resurrection process. The spiritually renewed mind also brings to our remembrance the effects of the Atonement—we really are not obliged any longer to obey the will of the flesh. We are no longer slaves to sin or the helpless automaton, relegated to the practice of unrighteous acts. We are the sons of God and as such are governed by a new Lord and motivated by a new set of guiding principles and participants in the Kingdom of God.

Since the natural world is blind to the principles and the Kingdom, it takes the wisdom and knowledge that comes through the second birth to guarantee our walk in the ways of the Kingdom of God. This demands that the heart and the spirit of man break the natural tendencies between them and produce the harmony necessary to maintain the believer in the Kingdom of God. There is a type of synergism created between the spirit and the soul of man that is astounding. Until the two agree, the body has no other alternative than to drift along in a duality that could, eventually, lead to death. John 3:5 is the key to understanding this concept:

> *...Verily, verily, I say unto thee, Except a man be born of water and of the Spirit, he cannot enter into the kingdom of God* (John 3:5).

Jesus tells us here that there are two kinds of births—the birth of water and the birth of the Spirit—and that each is necessary to enter the Kingdom of God. The first birth deals with sin and signifies cleansing from the impurities that are the residue of sin and unrighteousness. It is the first step in the process of entering into the Kingdom of God. This initial step only takes place as our spirits will to have intercourse with the Holy Spirit. The result of this union is a mind desiring to receive Jesus of Nazareth as the Christ of Heaven. This then releases the power, or the authority or permission, that causes us to become the sons of God. When we surrender our wills in faith to God, we are acknowledging His name, His character, His authority, and His divine nature.

Baptism in water is like the activity at the bronze laver in the Outer Court of the tabernacle. Before the outward sign of baptism is administered, the mind agrees to be cleansed. Baptism, like the cleansing that takes place at the laver, is representative of the decision the mind made to be free of all sin. Once the blinders of sin associated with the natural life have been removed from the mind, the believer is free to appreciate every nuance of the Kingdom of God.

Jesus proclaims and commands the need for the intimacy that comes with water baptism. He also proclaims and commands a second step, the birth that takes place through the Spirit.

Many who receive the birth by water remain satisfied with that Outer Court experience. They stop short of the fullness offered by the Lord. They will never appreciate the cooperation that takes place in the lives of those who go beyond the Outer Court, beyond water birth. Those who are content in the Outer Court remain outside observers of the Kingdom of God. To enter the Kingdom, one must be born of both water and the Spirit.

Religious spirits promote a life of stagnation. The life of those who remain at the brazen laver and fail to pursue the life awaiting them in the Holy Place, is stagnant. They may see or conceive of the notion of the Kingdom of God, but they cannot enter in. They have chosen to stop their spiritual progression. They have chosen to remain in the Outer Court, satisfied with half an experience, constantly battling sin and the life that was washed in the blood of the Lamb. Little do they know that the next step in the progression will lead them into a life where a choice between righteousness and sin is less problematic. The option we have to accept the second birth grants us entrance into the theology of Kingdom, but to actually set foot in the Kingdom demands a dual birth of water and the Spirit.

We must never settle for the crumbs of the spirit life. The second birth affords us the opportunity to walk in newness of life, which includes the blessings of the Kingdom life. But, we cannot realize the spiritual position awaiting us if we remain wedded to our first works. If we build a permanent habitation in the Outer Court, we will limit our fellowship with God to what He has done to cleanse us from the perils of sin. We will celebrate our initial encounter with God and assume that anything more is superfluous and unnecessary. Such a limited view of God's provision limits our knowledge of the Kingdom of God. It also denies us the opportunity to experience the Kingdom.

Many churches developed their dogma and their denominational creeds around the Outer Court experience. They argue and debate on the form of the Outer Court experience. They devise a set format and proclaim glowing words and phrases during this time of cleansing. But they have missed the mark and the purpose of the activity that should surround the brazen laver. The laver's true purpose is to deal forthrightly with our sin nature and to reckon it as dead. It exposes human attempts at restoration and personifies the atonement provided by the blood of Jesus Christ.

This is all pointing toward a fundamental truth. God the Father has a ritual in mind that is centered on a conscious relationship with Him. This is the relationship the first Adam had with the Father before his fall. There is less emphasis on external activity and more emphasis on personal interaction. There is more emphasis placed on yielding one's self to the agenda of God. The awareness of the flesh decreases as the Spirit of the living God fulfills His mission and purpose in the believer's life.

It is at this place where the spiritual inheritance and prowess of the born-again believer are confirmed. The gifts and anointing necessary for Kingdom pursuits are illuminated here. The reborn spirit is filled with an intense desire to walk in this Kingdom heritage. Everything is considered empty and without value compared to the splendor of the Kingdom. The habitual is interrupted. The static is agitated.

The joining of the water and the spiritual births produces the reality of walking in the Kingdom, not just a perception of the Kingdom. The coalescing of water and Spirit is intended to enlarge the borders of a believer's perspective and carry him beyond the mundane of earthly religion into the shores of the ethereal.

The water and the Spirit work together to invite the believer into a position where the spiritual is less foreboding and more *instinctive*. The born-again believer is given a new spiritual, genetic makeup that is radically different from those genes inherited from the biological birth. The believer's behavior changes as he reacts to the genetic pattern inherited from God as one of His begotten. John 3:6 confirms this concept:

Flesh gives birth to flesh but the Spirit gives birth to spirit (John 3:6 NIV).

Clearly, Jesus is saying that when we are born of the flesh, we can only expect that our behavior, thoughts, and perspectives will emanate from the realm of the flesh. Everything we do or perceive, think or create, will be birthed from a paradigm of flesh. It is ludicrous to expect anything different. The whole basis for the design, the scheme, the plan, and the strategy is that whatever is birthed from one given system, paradigm, or realm will, of necessity, consist of the patterns and makeup, and the nature and characteristics of that paradigm. It is an inescapable fact of multiplication and replication.

Jesus is confirming a simple reality. The flesh kingdom and the Kingdom of the Spirit work in much the same way. The things that are unique in the realm of the flesh will show up in natural, fleshly ways. The things that are unique in the realm of the spirit are manifested in the life of the person who is birthed from the Spirit. There is a travail that accompanies spiritual rebirth. The flesh has a force of its own and it uses this force in an attempt to abort the spiritual birth. But once the necessary death has occurred, the spiritual birth overcomes the wiles of the flesh and propels the believer into the Kingdom realm. This death to self causes anything that would impede the mind's abililty to accept fully the reality of the second birth to step aside. The flesh, in contrast, wants something to malfunction during the process of the labor and delivery of a spiritual birth.

Once we understand that a life that truly flows in the Spirit never takes place without resurrection, we will not be so hesitant about the death of our flesh. "Death" in the Greek is *thanatos*, which is defined as a separation of the soul (the spiritual part of man) from the body (the material part). In such a separation, the latter ceases to function and turns to dust. *Vine's* also defines death as man's separation from God. The word common to both definitions is the word *separation*. The process of being born again begins with the decision, prompted by the Holy Ghost, to allow the separation.

The call to separate is not to get us to merely stop activities that reek of unrighteousness. The call to separate is also the summons to discover the root of such behavior and to amputate it. The new behavior, separated from the old, is the product of a deeper motivation. To discover the internal source of unrighteous deeds is an important step in the process of separation. Unrighteous deeds are the products of fleshly motivations. As a new creation, we must allow the Holy Spirit to be the candle of the soul. We must allow Him to illuminate the hidden recesses of our inner man and expose the motivations, inducements, and preferences that influence our behavior. With the help of the Holy Spirit, we will be consistent rather than spiritually schizophrenic, subject to behavioral fluctuations. The root of those behavioral abnormalities must be exposed and uprooted through the work of the Holy Ghost.

There is a call to reality, a call to transparency, a call to be released from delusions and to come to an understanding of the source of our dysphoria. In order to deal with the source, we are given an arsenal of spiritual weapons to prevent the reemergence of unrighteous works in the future. We are commissioned to leave the shallow, muddy waters of the first order and to move into the deep, clear waters that God is calling us to enter. The newborn spirit is overwhelmed with desire to know the Father and this can only be accomplished through the revelation of the Holy Spirit. With the demise of normative religious thinking, the believer can cultivate his new nature as he wanders through the wonders God has laid before him. He can partake of a deep communion with the Father as he is filled with confidence to enter behind the veil into the Most Holy Place.

The superficiality of remaining in the Outer Court at the bronze laver is repulsive to one who has been truly born again. The waters of the Outer Court will not satisfy his thirst, a thirst that will only find relief in the presence of God. Once tasted, the believer realizes he is incomplete and hindered in his walk as long as he remains focused upon the work of the Outer Court. As he dies to the flesh and the genetic patterns of his spirit birth take control, he willingly follows the leading of the Holy Spirit into the Holy Place.

Remember, once the experience of the Outer Court ended, the priest separated himself from the multitude as he entered into the Holy Place. Then, he further separated himself as he entered the Most Holy Place, the Holy of Holies. Here he is in a place that is all God. There is no mixture whatsoever.

Only a select group of priests were permitted to minister to the Lord behind the veil. That privilege has now been extended to us because we have been made sons of God and part of the royal priesthood. Through our own death and separation, we have access to the presence of God. As we progress spiritually, the demand for separation increases. Any attempt to cling to the former system must be abandoned if we desire to move into the depths of the heart of God. When we are truly born again, the fundamentals of religion are of interest only if they serve as stepping stones into the fullness of God. Hebrews 6:1-2 in the King James Version helps us to understand this.

Therefore leaving the principles of the doctrine of Christ, let us go on unto perfection; not laying again the foundation of repentance from dead works, and of faith toward God, of the doctrine of baptisms, and of laying on of hands, and of resurrection of the dead, and of eternal judgment (Hebrews 6:1-2).

The inner nature of the born-again person drives him to progress in his pursuit of God. He is compelled to move beyond the superficial and to strive for maturity, to actually go on to perfection or wholeness. The fundamental beliefs of the new birth are identified and incorporated into the life of the believer. Every former belief is seen in light of the new birth and they are left behind as the believer, filled with urgency, strives to grow in the Lord. The sense of urgency emanates from a deep desire to move into an increasingly intimate relationship with the Father, an intimacy built upon this new set of fundamental principles. As the physical body grows in the earthly domain, so too does the spiritual body grow in the spiritual domain.

There is a type of violence that takes place in the transcendent process, but this is absolutely necessary to our walking wholeheartedly with the Lord. Hebrews 12:27-28 clarifies this.

And this word, Yet once more, signifieth the removing of those things that are shaken, as of things that are made, that those things which cannot be shaken may remain. Wherefore we receiving a kingdom which cannot be moved, let us have grace, whereby we may serve God acceptably with reverence and godly fear (Hebrews 12:27-28).

The Lord shakes all those things that are made or manufactured by the will and intelligence of men. That shaking truly begins with the spiritual baptism, the spiritual birth. Its purpose is to prepare each of us for our journey into the Most Holy Place, which is the unmovable Kingdom of God.

Chapter 8

Final Things

I trust that as you have journeyed through the intricacies of the second birth, your perspective of the truth of the born-again experience has been enhanced. I pray you will respond to this new understanding, which will positively affect your walk with the Lord for the rest of your life.

It is imperative, however, that we draw some conclusions as a result of our journey. It is important to summarize the practical spiritual truths the Holy Spirit intends to implement in our lives as we consider all that our minds have been exposed to through these pages.

First, only those who are seeking the deeper things of God will wander in the intricate caverns of the second birth. If they choose, they will discover within them a yearning to go deeper in their fellowship with the Lord. What they will soon realize is that even the desire for more is a product of the second birth. This kind of desire does not come from the cultural notions of traditional religion. The desire to answer the call of God, to draw near to Him in a richer way, does not result from a superficial engagement with the trappings of the mundane and the temporal. Essentially, one who is born again cannot help or avoid this yearning for the depth of God; it is in the spiritual genetic patterns one receives in the birthing process. If the Church is to move beyond the superficial, then she must remove the mystery, the half-truths, and the mythologies shrouding the born-again experience and allow the Holy Spirit to perform His work of guiding the Church into the truth of the born-again experience.

Second, the Church must realize that if we are to ever take the plunge into the depths of God, then we must allow ourselves to undergo a paradigm shift where the second birth is concerned. We must open ourselves to the liberating truth that God often annuls the first order to establish the second. He does this because historically the first has brought man to a certain point, but becomes ineffective in completing the task set aside and ordained by God. John the Baptist was born before Jesus the Christ. John's purpose was to herald Christ's coming. He was not the ultimate or the end of God's plan. The end of the plan was Jesus Christ. John fulfilled his purpose, but he also recognized his status as the forerunner to the King of kings. He walked with confidence in the divine assurance of his purpose.

The Church, then, is called to look carefully at our interpretation of the second birth. It is required to realize that our watered-down religious version lacks potency. It must allow the people to undergo a paradigm shift that will draw them into the labyrinth of liberating knowledge regarding the second birth.

Third, the second birth allows us to be set free from familial iniquity and thought patterns that would hinder our walk in the spiritual abundance the Lord offers. Through the second birth God has placed dreams and purposes within us. They are realized even though our natural birth has placed us in less than fortuitous circumstances. The second birth allows each of us to take the superlatives as well as the atrocities of our past and use them to the glory of God. Neither is able to control or influence us any longer because they must succumb to the power and the authority of the second birth. With that rebirth, the gifts that lie dormant within each one of us burst forth into full bloom. A mind, once paralyzed and filled with fear of failure and defeat, is renewed. The belief that we are unproductive and that our dreams are unattainable because of our social status, family history, or cultural baggage, is disabled. Now we fully understand the efficacy of the second birth in our lives. The proclamation that we are a new creation is true. Old things have indeed passed away and behold, "all things are become new" (2 Cor. 5:17)!

Fourth, the second birth changes our life styles. We receive a renewed mind, the mind Adam had before he fell. This new mind is the mind of Christ. With this in mind, we are able to declare, like Jesus, that we only do what we see the Father do and we only say what we hear the Father says (see Jn. 5:19,30). Our behavior and thought processes are revolutionized because our thoughts are no longer our own. They emanate from the very throne room of God. The new mind draws us deeper into the Father and His Word so that, as His Word offers examples of godly behavior, our minds accept the example and follow it. As His Word outlines His thoughts, then our minds, through spiritual revelation, delight in the flow from God's imagination. Our renewed mind allows us to focus in on the voice of God so we mimic His Word. We go back to the original. We are swept back in time to a place of ultimate fellowship with the Lord. The shroud of carnality is removed as we are resurrected to walk in the Spirit. It is the renewed mind, the mind of God, that substitutes for the carnal, excuse-offering mind of our natural state. We are consumed as we become one with the Father. We become saturated with His words and we reside in the core of His purpose. Our lives are established upon complete obedience to the will of God and we are preoccupied with replicating what we have seen the Father do through our intimate fellowship with Him.

Fifth, the second birth causes us to move beyond the boundaries of church into the endless parameters of God's Kingdom. It is here, in a new time and place, that we submit to the reign of the Lord. This comes through chaos. Often times, the traditional mind-set reacts violently against the effort of our spirits to push us to accept the paradigm of Kingdom. The second birth allows us to conceptualize and enter the Kingdom of God. We release our minds from the confines of church culture and seek the vistas of God where He reigns in His Kingdom.

That is the second birth—powerful, life-changing, revolutionary. Only a few will walk in its glory. Please join with me on this journey into our second birth. Together we will find the potential and the determination to walk with the King of kings!